Do The
RIGHT
THING

D1255757

Do the Right Thing:

A Surgeon's Approach to Life

by

Arthur Lauretano, M.D., M.S., F.A.C.S.

ENTShred Media

First Edition

ISBN: 978-0-9976360-0-0

DEDICATION

To my patients, from whom I have learned so much: I hope you have benefited from my care. I have tried my best for you.

To my wife Adrienne, whom I love with all my heart: You are my rock when I need support, my pillow when I need rest, my best friend when I need comfort. Thank you for putting up with me – thank you for loving me.

To my kids, Danielle and Arthur, Jr., whom I truly love and cherish as my greatest treasures: You guys keep me young. I'm glad you share my crazy and unique sense of humor.

To my parents, who taught me the meaning of integrity: I love you too. Thanks for everything.

To Keith Garde, who encouraged me to write this book: You are inspirational, more than you will know.

To all the teachers and mentors, particularly Mrs. Rose Lester, Brother Fred Eid, and Doctor William Silen. To my cousins Andrea Phelan (teacher extraordinaire) for her contributions to teaching, and Greg Natola (guitarist extraordinaire) for his contributions to my guitar playing. To my karate instructors Asa Seeley and Evan Pantazi, who taught me the path to balance. To Jo Shapiro, M.D., my former associate, and Bjorn Bie, M.D., my senior partner: You are my current mentors, whether you realize it or not.

To my band mate Dave Yarin: We are brothers from different mothers. Thanks for sharing my obsession and compassion for guitar playing. Thanks for putting up with my insanity.

To my associates, Doctors Bjorn Bie, Samir Bhatt, Vijay Nayak, and Eric Stein: Thanks for your support and for taking such good care of our patients. Thanks for putting up with my antics. You guys are great doctors.

To Patty Kenney, my secretary, who finds order in the chaos and sanity amidst the insanity, and leads me through the maze that is my work schedule.

To Joe Erickson, my therapist: You have elevated listening from a skill to an art form. Thanks for being there for me.

To everyone at Lowell General Hospital: Thanks for all the wonderful opportunities you have given me.

To those who believed in me: Thank you for the support. To those who didn't believe in me: Thank you for the motivation.

Disclaimer

The ideas, opinions, and concepts this book presents are the opinions of Arthur M. Lauretano, M.D., M.S., F.A.C.S., and do not represent the opinions of my current associates (Mass. ENT Associates), or my former practice (The Joint Center for Otolaryngology), or any of the institutions, hospitals, professional societies or organizations with which I am or have been affiliated (including teaching and residency affiliations). Finally, the cases I present have been modified to protect patient confidentiality, while retaining enough of the original content to make my points.

TABLE OF CONTENTS

FOREWORD

I'll never forget the first day I met Arthur Lauretano. It was a bitter cold winter in Boston. I was in my third year of medical school, and I had decided to do an elective month in Otolaryngology (Ear, Nose, and Throat Surgery) at two busy teaching hospitals. This was the month I'd make my decision about whether I'd chose this field as my future. I called Arthur on his pager the night before the rotation, and he suggested we meet in the hospital lobby at 6 a.m. the next day. At 6 on the nose, in came Arthur Lauretano, already having had quite a morning and previous night in the operating room. "OK, let's go!" he said without looking back. We realized he was someone to follow, literally and figuratively. This guy was fast, but he never made anyone — patient, student, nurse, or colleague — feel rushed. How did he do that? As he moved through the quiet hospital halls in the dark morning hours, the tails of his long white coat flew. This was his super-hero cape.

In the weeks ahead, we learned so much from Arthur. There was rarely time to sit down for a lecture, but his leading us by example, doing the right thing without a second thought, carried invaluable lessons. I remember a chronically ill elderly woman with severe lung and tracheal (windpipe) disease. She was royalty (a princess) from across many oceans. Her room comprised nearly the entire hospital wing, with her private doctors, family members, and a room fruit baskets, refreshed daily. Arthur led us into her room to "take a listen to the royal lungs." Down the hall, an IV drug abuser had developed a neck abscess from skin popping (a technique used by IV drug users when they have no usable veins). Arthur treated him with as much respect, time, and care as he did the VIP down the hall. Patients were patients, and they needed his help.

ARTHUR LAURETANO

Between the royal lungs and skin popping patient, my time in those busy hospitals under Arthur's tutelage confirmed my choice of otolaryngology. He was not just an ear, nose, and throat doctor. He was a doctor, a human being, a teacher. We didn't need a blackboard and a classroom to see it.

I worked with Arthur as my senior resident, and later, as my attending. He was always Arthur. He worked as hard, had the same respect for all around him, and always gave his all at all times. He was selfless, and had an unprecedented sense of humor, perspective, and honesty.

I'll never forget being in the operating room when I was a senior resident and he was a new attending surgeon. We were operating on a neck, and we couldn't stop the bleeding—not one big blood vessel, but a lot of what we call diffuse bleeding. We worked methodically to stop any bleeder we could see, but to no avail. Until the bleeding just stopped. Like that. And then the wise words: "You know, Nina, bleeding like that is sometimes like a traffic jam. It's a big mess, and then it's fine. Sometimes you never know the reason for the bloody mess, or why the traffic was there in the first place. But when it's gone, it doesn't seem to matter." Living in Los Angeles, where traffic is part of life, and doing lots of neck surgery, where diffuse bleeding occurs all the time, I still think of this and remember those wise words. Sometimes things just get better.

Over 20 years later, I still learn from Arthur Lauretano. This book has countless lessons about what doing the right thing means to him and to me, and what it can mean to you. You might wonder, how can a surgeon, or someone in a field so narrow as Ear, Nose, and Throat Surgery, discuss an approach to life? You will find that much of a doctor's life can be translated to life in general.

Much of this book is about perspective—how to define ability, success, failure, talent, work ethic, and happiness. Everyone may define these differently. There are common metrics. How do you reach your potential? How do you stay positive when life is chaotic?

This book opened my eyes to what is right in front of me—the value of my and other people's time, and a chance to see things from others' eyes. Perspective. When patients run late, I need to realize they probably tried to be on time. Perhaps their child had an exam at school, there was traffic on the freeway, or even traffic in our parking lot! When I run late, I need to understand a patient's anger, be transparent, and try to rectify the situation, so we can start off on the right foot. I meet new patients every day, and first impressions are key to a relationship based on trust.

Arthur emphasizes social status. As doctors, we're no better or worse than those in other professions. We are no better than those who cannot work. Just because our patient may be royalty, she is no better than the man with an IV-drug-related illness. My practice is a few miles from Hollywood, so we see our share of movie and TV stars, but all patients deserve the same VIP treatment.

Success is a recurring theme in this book. It has its own chapter but it is woven throughout. It's easy to define success—graduations, honors, high test scores, competitive graduate programs, and prestigious jobs. But then life hits, and the kudos blurs. Is the world-renowned cardiac surgeon whose marriage fell apart because he was never there for his wife and kids a success? Is the CEO who built an empire, only to see his children squander their riches, a success? What about my fifth-grade teacher who keeps in touch with 30 years' worth of students, many of whom remember every artist and musician she taught us? Is she a success? Or the woman who gave up her career as a corporate lawyer to raise her children.

Success or failure? We all have successes, but also carry failures. And this is okay. This book made me realize one reason we go on is that nobody is a complete success or failure. A lot depends on how we define these. Not how others do.

This book gives you many opportunities to do the right thing in your life. Many of us do the right thing without a second thought. But we need reminders about who we are, what is of value, and how to make a positive impact in many ways, for many people. After re-reading this book I feel rejuvenated in how I approach my work, family, friends, and even my alone time. The book suggests opportunities that though trivial, can have tremendous impacts on others. A small, caring gesture may seem insignificant but profound to the recipient. Don't underestimate the impact of doing the right thing.

Nina Shapiro, M.D., Professor of Otolaryngology at UCLA and author of *Take a Deep Breath*.

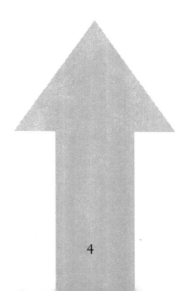

INTRODUCTION

How did I, a surgeon, decide to write a self-help book about my approach to life? Why is it called *A Surgeon's Approach* and not *The Surgeon's Approach* or even *One Surgeon's Approach?*

This book did not start out as a self-help book. I am an ENT (Ear, Nose, and Throat) surgeon and I treat a lot of patients for snoring. Over a sushi dinner one night, my friend Keith mentioned that I must have a lot of interesting stories about snoring. I explained there was only one story. One person snores, and if I don't fix the problem, the bed partner wants to kill the snorer.

The more interesting stories, I told him, may lie in the questions people ask me about my job: How do you keep smiling when seeing between 30 and 40 patients a day? How do you stand in the OR (operating room) for six hours straight during a long cancer surgery? How do you drive into the hospital for an emergency tracheotomy at 2 a.m. and be able to function with a clear head and without falling asleep? How do you tell people they are going to die from their cancer?

I explained that what distinguishes a career from a job is that you never stop thinking about your career. We often believe we are our career. In my case, I am always a doctor. I sometimes forget to turn that off.

I gave Keith an example:

One night I came home just in time for dinner with my family. I had been in the operating room all day and had performed thyroidectomies (removal of a diseased thyroid gland) on three patients. You've probably seen plenty of television shows where the doctors ask the scrub nurse or tech to pass various instruments: "knife," "suction," "retractor," "clamp."

Surgeons are taught to never let our eyes leave the surgical field. In thyroid surgery my eyes are glued to the three-inch-by-three-inch opening in the neck. A lot can happen in a split second, particularly bleeding. So we ask for a piece of equipment quickly and with minimal words. "Please" and "Thank you" are understood. At supper, after three thyroidectomies, my mind was filled with "knife," "bovie," "nerve stimulator," "hemostat," and so on.

So at dinner, my eyes glued to my steak, I reached across the table and said clearly and authoritatively, "Knife."

My wife and kids looked at me. "What?" they said in shocked tones.

"Knife," I repeated with a bit more conviction.

My family started laughing. "Get your own knife," they said, and, "You're not in the OR anymore."

Later, talking with Keith, manager of a major music act, I said that many aspects of my work ethic and approach to my career impact other things.

I play guitar, and my wife won me a trip to Rock and Roll Fantasy Camp. The week before the trip, I stayed up until 2 a.m., practicing Aerosmith's "Living on the Edge," Deep Purple's "Highway Star," and Led Zeppelin's "The Ocean." The morning of the audition, I practiced for another three hours in my hotel room to make sure I knew every note. I apply the same intensity to my surgical career. I review my cases the night before every surgery and, in the morning, go over every X-ray and lab, review very detail, and run every step in my head. That compulsiveness is important in a surgeon and in an accountant (as a patient once told me), but I have often blurred my approach to work and leisure.

This is not necessarily bad. My attitude toward many things—work or play—is the same because I am driven by a level of compulsiveness I see in a lot of physicians, and a passion for what I do and *compassion* for the people I treat. The ideal result in medicine is a happy, healthy patient. As a head and neck cancer surgeon, I find that is not always possible. I may simply be able to keep a terminal cancer patient comfortable or keep one alive to see his daughter married or grandchild born (both true stories).

Keith and I considered writing a book about how my career influenced my approach to life. We found that some principles could be applied to many situations, from daily occurrences at home to global scenarios.

Some of my approaches may differ from those of other physicians. So I decided to call this book *A Surgeon's Approach to Life* instead of *The Surgeon's Approach to Life*.

I promise to be honest. If I present a real patient story (without names and identifying data) I will let you know. If a story is hypothetical, I will let you know, though even these are based on real cases. Some of my opinions may surprise you. They may go against your preconceptions of doctors and surgeons.

You may not expect a book on an approach to life to be written by a surgeon. After all, in medical school surgeons are known for wanting to cut first and ask questions later, and entering the anatomy lab with a scalpel in one hand and a roast beef sandwich in the other. In psychiatry class, we tried to get the lowest grade without failing because we didn't want to show our softer side.

I heard the following story in medical school and saw it on the front page of the *Wall Street Journal*, I believe:

An internist, a psychiatrist, and a surgeon are duck hunting. They decide to take turns shooting to see who can get the first duck. After drawing straws, the internist goes first, then the psychiatrist, then the surgeon. A flock of birds flies overhead. The internist aims his gun, then says, "They look like ducks, but they could be geese or pheasants, and we are specifically hunting ducks. I'd like to run some tests, get a few X-rays, some labs, and then determine if these are ducks before I shoot." He never fires a shot, and the birds fly off.

Another flock flies by. It is the psychiatrist's turn. He aims his gun, then says, "These birds display the characteristic behavioral patterns typical of ducks. The configuration of the flock speaks to the structural organization I would expect to see in a community of ducks, and their direction speaks to their desire for food and shelter. However, similar behavior can be seen in geese and pheasants, so I would like to conduct some interviews and have a few sessions with these birds to see if, in fact, they are ducks." He never fires a shot, and the birds fly off.

It is now the surgeon's turn. He stands up with his gun raised and pointed at the sky before any birds are even in view. A flock of birds approaches. As soon as the birds are in range, the surgeon opens fire, blasting away at the birds until his gun is empty. Feathers fly everywhere, and birds fall from the sky like rain. When his gun is empty, he walks up to one of the dead birds, picks it up, and turns to the other two doctors. "Yup, it's a duck!"

For years, this has been the surgeon's view. "Cut first; ask questions later." "A chance to cut is a chance to cure." "When in doubt, cut it out." "Nothing heals like cold steel."

This is extreme, and surgeons pride themselves on a full knowledge of medicine and the technical prowess required to perform complicated surgery. We are compassionate and care about our patients. But most of my medical colleagues would expect a psychiatrist, internist, pediatrician, or family practitioner to write this kind of book, not a surgeon. This is one of the reasons I called this book *A Surgeon's Approach to Life*. Perhaps I am just a little (or a lot) different from my surgical colleagues.

How did I come up with the title *Do the Right Thing?* I've used this line often in medicine and life. If my daughter asks if she should work on her school project or go to a concert, I'll say, "Do the right thing," then let her consider what the right thing is. I want her to do her schoolwork, but I love the cryptic tone in "Do the right thing."

This phrase has important implications. It suggests there is at least one possibility that is the right thing, that will improve the situation. It also assumes we understand the concept of "right," whether it's the right medical or surgical treatment, or deciding to approach a bully at school. It could be deciding to follow an honest, but perhaps more difficult path at work. Finally, telling someone in earnest to "Do the right thing" implies you believe he has the skills, knowledge, work ethic, and principles to understand the possibilities, recognize the importance of the situation, and know right from wrong. You are confident he has the ability to "Do the right thing." This final concept is the reason for the title.

In my first month of residency, I had a complicated case—an elderly patient with an increased heart rate (tachycardic). She had had surgery and there were multiple possible reasons for the problem. Thanks to my medical school training at Boston University and particularly at Boston City Hospital, I'd gained a lot of patient experience. Could the problem be from pain or from hypovolemia (inadequate amount of fluid given intravenously compared to fluids lost during surgery)? Did she have heart problems? I assessed the patient and called my senior resident.

As a medical student at BU, I'd heard the adages: "See one, do one, teach one" and "Feel free to call (i.e., for help), but remember, calling is a sign of weakness!" My first night on call as a surgical intern, I'd managed a very sick patient by myself, and I learned quickly that these adages were *not* acceptable at Beth Israel Hospital. When I presented my management to the senior residents, they were angry that I hadn't called anyone for help.

So this time I called the senior resident and went through each possible diagnosis and my treatment options. He said, "Do the right thing." I thought, I get chewed out for not calling, then get an enigmatic response when I do call. Yet this resident trusted me, let me help in the OR, and praised me in front of other attendings (attending physicians).

Then I understood. In saying "Do the right thing," the resident wasn't trying to be mysterious. He saw I had carefully considered everything that could be wrong with the patient. He trusted I had the knowledge and skills to make the right treatment decisions. In this way he was also "Doing the right thing."

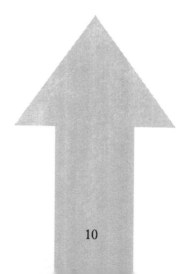

Chapter One:
FIRST IMPRESSIONS

You never get a second chance to make a first impression. This may sound like a cliché but it applies to my interactions with patients. I'm in the office about half the week, and I see between 30 and 40 patients a day. The rest of the time I'm in the operating room. I'm on call every fifth week. At least a third of my patient encounters are with people I'm meeting for the first time. It is essential for me to make a good first impression. I'll start with an example of my making a poor first impression.

False Starts

I'd started my call week on Friday morning. At 4 a.m. on Saturday, a patient called with bleeding after a tonsillectomy—not an unexpected complication. Each time I'd spoken to the patient, I'd suggested we meet at the hospital so I could operate to stop the bleeding. Each time she'd refused, and this began to weigh heavily on me. At 6 a.m., I was called to check a patient with a severe sore throat. Then I had rounds at the hospital, and saw patients in the office from 9 a.m. to noon. I couldn't get in touch with my tonsillectomy patient. She could be having significant blood loss; we might be losing precious time. Then the hospital called with an inpatient with intermittent, profuse bleeding from her nose. Nasal packing had slowed the bleeding, but not stopped it. I ran to the hospital, still preoccupied with the tonsillectomy patient.

I met the nosebleed patient and her two daughters and explained that, since everything else had been done to stop the bleeding, it was best to take her to the OR to cauterize the vessel. I explained this carefully, but I was more matter-of-fact than usual. The patient's daughters saw that my mind was elsewhere and assumed I was annoyed at being called in to see their mother. One said sarcastically, "I'm sorry we had to drag you away from your golf game on a Saturday morning." I explained how long I'd been working, and was upset because of problems with another patient. But they didn't want to hear that, especially as I was about to operate on their mother. Though I resolved the patient's problem, I didn't exactly get any "positive vibes" from her family.

Getting off to a bad start harms the patient-doctor relationship. We learn in medical school and residency that good patient-doctor rapport helps patients trust their doctors, comply with the treatment plan, and feel they can call with questions, concerns, or emergencies. From a medico-legal standpoint, doctors are much less likely to get sued when there is good rapport.

> *You never get a second chance to make a first impression.*

My appearance, my demeanor, and my attentiveness all factor into patients' first impressions. As an ear, nose, and throat surgeon, I see a lot of children. So I have to make a good first impression on the parents and the children. If those kids see me as a big, scary monster, I'm not going to get very far. So I check for monkeys in their ears. When I need to look inside the nose, I lift it up to make them look like a pig. To check their throat, I ask them to open their mouth like a lion.

We all have opportunities to make first impressions. Whether it's at work or leisure, coaching our kid's soccer team, or shopping at the local supermarket, opportunities arise all the time.

Try Again

Let's say you go to the local coffee shop and the person who serves you is new. He's pleasant, listens to your order, gets it right, and the coffee is delicious. You're probably going to go back the next day. Let's say you go to the same place, but the person behind the counter is talking to his co-worker and barely pays attention to you. You ask for a large French vanilla hot coffee with milk and three Equals, but

> *Our appearance, our attitude, our confidence, our punctuality, our level of preparation all contribute to a winning first impression.*

he starts making an iced decaf. You explain nicely that he's not making the right order, he looks annoyed, and finally gets it right. The coffee is still delicious, but I suspect you're a little less likely to make this your regular morning stop.

This is just coffee, but the first impression for a business deal, a major purchase, or an important presentation is very important. Our appearance, our attitude, our confidence, our punctuality, our level of preparation all contribute to a winning first impression. Yet how often do we pay attention to these details? Also, have you ever considered how many first impressions you get to make in a single day?

I see about 10 new patients a day, as well as new family members of current patients. Since I'm going to be providing their health care, I need to be pleasant, confident, approachable, and a good listener–someone they can confide in who is not judgmental. You may think, "He's a surgeon. Of course this is important. But how does this apply to me?"

The importance of making a good first impression applies whatever we do. In interviews, in retail, and public service, every new customer is a first impression. A good first impression makes our job easier, our attitude better, and our life happier.

My wife is a homemaker who works 24/7 at home with the kids. When she meets someone who's working on our house, she has to present herself as someone with whom the contractor wants to work, and *vice versa*. Our son has a learning disability. We've met with multiple therapists and school personnel to set up plans for him. Sometimes we've been frazzled or defensive during these interactions. Sometimes the service providers haven't been in the best frame of mind. When the initial interaction was poor, subsequent ones were extremely difficult. Even when we rectified the poor first impression, follow-ups were more strained and it took longer to establish rapport.

Two-way Streets

Do patients make a first impression on me? Absolutely. I learn a lot in that first encounter. Take the example of a child and his parents consulting on ear tubes for recurrent infections. Here are examples of ways the interactions may go. based on what I've encountered in my practice. In both cases, the patient is a cooperative four-year-old, so the child is not an issue.

Example 1. A pleasant mother reviews her child's medical history, explains the pediatrician has recommended ear tubes, and wants to know more. We have a comfortable conversation about how the child is hearing in preschool, the TV shows he likes, and so on. We discuss the ear tubes procedure, surgery logistics, and follow-up visits. The mother signs a consent form. This is her first child and the child's first surgery. I explain it is normal to be nervous, and I will be available for questions or concerns. I give her a printed information sheet and a copy of the signed consent form.

Example 2. The father is texting. I introduce myself. He continues to text, and interacts little while I examine the child. We discuss the procedure, risks, and so on, but this time it's more of an explanation than a discussion. Some doctors would ask the father to come back when he's ready to talk.

The father has not made a good impression on me. I have no way of knowing if he gets it. Will he make sure the child's stomach is empty before surgery? Will he take the child to the postoperative visits? In this case I recommend surgery but ask the father to review the printed information and the consent form. I also ask him to return for another appointment to make sure he understands the surgery and why we are proceeding with it. I do this because I'm uncomfortable with my first impression.

One patient, while signing the consent form, asked me if she could still sue me even if she signed the form. Her surgery to remove a neck mass went well, but she faked a left-arm injury related to how her arm was positioned in the OR, and claimed her ulnar nerve was damaged. Nerve testing showed she was malingering—the medical term for faking it. I should have

The first impression is a two-way street, a mutual exchange.

trusted my first impression and asked myself whether it was wise to operate on someone who was discussing a malpractice suit. The first impression is a two-way street, a mutual exchange, in many respects no different from a first date—I try not to get my tie in my drink, and you try not to break your heel dancing.

Some patients will not come back after a single poor first impression. You may not get a chance to make a second impression. If I make a bad first impression, I do my best to apologize and explain, being honest, transparent, and humble. I want each patient to feel she's the most important person.

I respect people's time. Punctuality is an important part of the first impression. However, because I listen to my patient's entire story, I often run behind in my office. Many patients, especially those with cancer, have long, complex histories. I schedule those patients later in the day so I can spend unlimited time. Patients know that though I may run behind, they will not be rushed out.

I'm optimistic that in most cases, any of us can make up for a bad first impression. Make the second one count. If the first impression was good, don't be complacent. You've set a bar you have to clear in subsequent encounters.

Learning from Mistakes

When people don't give me a second chance, I take stock of what may have gone wrong and look at what I can learn. As I've heard at the American School of Karate, where I am a second-degree black belt in Kyusho-Kempo, "When you lose, don't lose the lesson." This comes from the teachings of the Dalai Lama—it's the second of the 18 "Instructions for Life."

Making a first impression is easy if you do the right things. Don't try to be something you're not. You don't need to wear a lab coat if you are a musician auditioning for a part, and I shouldn't walk in with ripped jeans and a ripped t-shirt if I'm Chief of Surgery at a major academic institution.

I want my patients to want a second encounter with me. So I try to answer all their questions. When I'm stressed I've sometimes said privately to my staff, "Man, I hate this job!" I don't want to project that to my patients, so I do a little pantomime ritual. I pretend I'm wearing a frown, then search my pockets and say, "Here it is." I put my hand over my mouth, then remove it to reveal a big smile.

Make each first impression as good, as great, as you can possibly make it!

Second Chances: The Reward

When people make a bad first impression on me, I consider their possible circumstances and give them a second chance. Very late one afternoon a man came in with a bad sore throat. We suggested seeing him another day, but the patient explained he'd already been treated with antibiotics and wasn't getting better. My staff felt he was a bit pushy. But I needed to do the right thing. I gave him a second chance. Something about him told me told me he had cancer. He opened his mouth and proved my intuition correct. He had a left tonsil cancer. I biopsied him right then and there, and we quickly got him into our cancer system for treatment. I was glad I gave him a second chance. He was pushy because he was scared.

In 1999 my son became ill. (I won't go into the background here.) His stomach shut down and for the next six months he had to have a feeding tube. At one point when he was not tolerating the tube, we were concerned he might die. Fortunately, I recalled a bit of wisdom from my internship and gave him Pedialyte to see if he could absorb it. (Thank you, Dr. William Silen, for teaching me about "dumping syndrome," and thank you, Pedialyte.) After six months he was able to be fed orally. He's now 17 and eats like nothing ever happened to him.

I tell you this because I went to work like many parents whose kids are ill. In spite of how much I hurt inside, in spite of the toll this was taking on me. I made sure that with each patient I made a good first impression. I saw kids for ear tubes and wondered if my son would reach their age. I tried to keep my patients from knowing that something bad was going on at home. I gave them my all. I would rather take a leave of absence than not perform at my best.

A Chinese proverb says, "Don't be over self-confident with your first impressions of people." First impressions are about more than appearance; they're about our attitudes, the words we say, our body language, and so on. Approach each encounter as a new chance to make a first impression. When we strive to make a good first impression and give second chances, we establish rapport and can build a lasting and productive relationship. Relationships of respect help us be good listeners, celebrate our uniqueness, help others, and make the world a better place. It's not the first impression we make, but the lasting impression we leave, that really matters. When we pay attention to the impressions we make and give others the chance to put their best foot forward on the first or even second try, we do the right thing.

> *It's not the first impression we make, but the lasting impression we leave, that really matters.*

Chapter Two:
TALENTS AND ABILITIES

Ralph Waldo Emerson said, "Every man I meet is in some way my superior." I love this quotation, because even before I'd found it, I'd been practicing it for years.

Although doctors have probably dropped a bit in the social hierarchy over the last few years, we're still generally well respected in our communities. Many people want their sons or daughters to be doctors, or marry doctors. I'm happy I can help people as a physician and that I can make an income that allows my family to have a comfortable home, live in a community with good schools, and participate in the activities we want to enjoy. But I don't think I'm better than anyone. I believe that most physicians share this perspective.

Building Rapport

I generally introduce myself to a patient as Arthur Lauretano. It drives some of my colleagues crazy that I don't use "Dr." The patient knows I'm the doctor. Arthur M. Lauretano, M.D., F.A.C.S. is written on my door and lab coat. My staff tells the patient that Dr. Lauretano will be right in. To me, it's more important they see me as a regular guy with whom they can feel comfortable and in whom they can confide. I don't believe that saying I'm Dr. Lauretano is a critical part of that first impression. I earn their trust by taking good care of them and showing them I'm knowledgeable, caring, and confident.

Part of my rapport with my patients is getting to know them, not just their illness or disease. "The good physician treats the disease; the great physician treats the patient who has the disease" (Sir William Osler). I want my patients to feel comfortable talking to me about their kids' problems or issues that go beyond the scope of an ENT practice. One patient is writing his life story. Each time he finishes a chapter, he sends it to me. Patients who are singers or musicians bring me their CDs or talk about performances. I'm a huge soccer fan and have a great time discussing games with my soccer-fan patients. Such encounters help me treat the whole patient. They feel comfortable talking with me, so we can develop a treatment plan that makes us all comfortable.

Remember Your Roots

I grew up in Medford, Massachusetts, a suburb of Boston—a primarily blue-collar, low-middle to middle-class community of about 60,000. It's about 80% Italian and Irish, with an African-American section. My father is a carpenter, my mother a housewife, and I'm an only child. Pretty much everyone in my huge Italian family is or was in the trades: plumbers, carpenters, electricians, pipefitters, and laborers.

I was always a good student and found a bit of an athletic niche in soccer. My real non-academic talent was music. I started on drums but couldn't afford a drum set, so began to play guitar on a hand-me-down from one of my cousins. I went to public school through eighth grade and took violin, upright bass, and orchestra. I did the usual jobs kids did: raking leaves and shoveling snow. I accompanied my dad on some side jobs he did for extra money when the carpenters' union was on strike. A few people had cash, and they had expensive clothes, but most of us wore things we got at the local factory outlet. I felt bad if my parents had to pay for fancy clothes for me.

I was accepted at MIT and Harvard for biomedical engineering, but I was also accepted into the Boston University Six-Year Medical Program. I wanted to finish medical school early and save my parents some tuition money, so I went to Boston University (BU). I gravitated to those from similar backgrounds. We all worked to pay our tuition (I worked in an emergency room as an orderly from high school through medical school). We felt fortunate about our abilities and opportunities so worked as hard as possible to make the most of them. I went on to do a residency in ENT at Harvard, then stayed in an academic practice at Harvard for three-and-a-half years before moving to private practice in the Greater Lowell, Massachusetts, area.

From high school through residency, I played in bands. I used to study for medical school tests during set breaks when we were playing clubs in the 1980s. I still play in a band with guys I've known for years. I coached my daughter's soccer team, got my national coaching license, and got back to playing soccer myself (until I killed my knee). I also took up martial arts and I am a second-degree black belt in Kyusho-Kempo Karate.

Understanding and Respect

Why all the history? I was blessed by God (or by fate, or luck, or Karma—whatever higher power you believe in) with talents and abilities. I had support from my family and live in a country that gives us great opportunities. I applied myself and worked hard. My background, education, work ethic, associations with others, and interests help me relate to others. I recognize that those with different talents are not inferior. This has helped me greatly in my career and in life in general.

In my first year or so of academic practice we had a very sick patient on the ward service with a deep neck infection. He was not getting better with antibiotics. The residents sensed he needed surgery. The patient was a professional blues singer and petrified he'd lose his voice box. I discovered he had necrotizing fasciitis of the neck—flesh-eating disease. I explained the severity of the situation, the need for aggressive surgery, and the potential for death. He begged me not to do anything that would injure his vocal cords, so I adjusted my approach to avoid this. The residents had told him that I was a guitar player and had treated a lot of musicians, so he was glad to have me as his surgeon. The patient pulled through and did well. A few months later, he got married at the House of Blues (at that time in Cambridge, Mass.), and invited me to attend and play after the ceremony. I played a whole set with him and later recorded a guitar solo on one of his CDs (a song about my saving his life). I could relate to him, his concerns, and specific needs, because of my experience in the music business.

> *I recognize that those with different talents are not inferior.*

Many issues can arise in large families. I have relatives on welfare. Some have battled substance abuse, and some have died trying. Some have smoked so long they developed end-stage lung disease and now depend on oxygen. When I see patients with substance abuse issues, I respond with compassion. We can't change the past. I stand by them as we fight their disease. At no point do I feel I am better than them, and at no point am I judgmental.

Do the Right Thing

As a medical student, I sometimes stayed late on the wards to talk to my patients, particularly my intravenous-drug-abuse patients. One drug abuser showed me how he found a vein. This made it easier for me to start his IVs. By the time I finished my rotations at Boston City Hospital, I could start an IV in anyone. I also learned how poor some patients' support systems were, and how important it was to understand this in order to treat the whole patient and ensure compliance with the treatment plan. In this day and age of trying to rein in medical costs, holistic plans are essential.

How does this apply to other aspects of my life? It drives me crazy when people talk down to others because of their job. I hate the expression, "If you don't focus on your studies, you'll be flipping burgers the rest of your life." Think about the person who is flipping burgers. Maybe academics weren't his thing. I asked the kid who works at the hospital coffee shop, "Do you ever take a day off?" He said he works as much as possible to save money for college. He's a hard worker. I always give him a big tip. Kids like that deserve a reward for their motivation.

In my last year of residency, I played a hospital party with my band. Someone at the party commented in a derogatory way, "Arthur's in his element now." What does that mean? Is there something wrong with playing in a band? My point is that we have different strengths, talents, and abilities. I respect you for who you are.

My daughter just finished art school. She's an animator. People often ask me if she's "pre-med." When I tell them she went to art school, some wonder if I am disappointed. I'm happy she's an animator. She's a very talented artist, right brain oriented, and definitely in the right profession for her. I will be disappointed if she doesn't put her best foot forward and make the most of her abilities. My son is 17 and wants to be an illustrator. I am happy he wants to go to art school, and I am encouraging him to be the best illustrator he can be. I am happy he wants to go to art school, and I am encouraging him to be the best character designer he can be.

I take care of a lot of injured wrestlers and basketball players who want to return to their sport as soon as possible. Because of my martial arts training, I can relate to their injuries, and consider ways we can get them back sooner. I don't say, "I'm the doctor; no sports for you for six weeks, no matter what." I help them formulate a plan that fits into what's important to them.

I'm proud to treat the school janitor who sees me every six months to check his nose and ears. I don't look down at the patient who can't work and is on welfare. Circumstances have made it hard for her to get on her feet. I'm not going to look down on that. I've seen it in my own family.

When we allow each other to put our talents and expertise to good use, we're doing the right thing.

"Every man I meet is in some way my superior." I enjoy learning from those with more expertise than I have, whether it's in medicine, a hobby, or an outside interest. We strive to improve ourselves, but also need understand our weaknesses. Over the years, I've done fewer complicated ear surgeries because I have colleagues who are more talented in that area. Sending such patients to them is doing the right thing.

In medical school, it's important to shine on rounds—to answer the attending's questions before everyone else does. This makes us competitive, and I'm not sure we ever get out of that mode, even when we're not at work.

When we recognize and respect each other's talents, we live in a much healthier environment. Mutual respect makes us productive as a society and the world a better place. When we allow each other to put our talents and expertise to good use, we're doing the right thing.

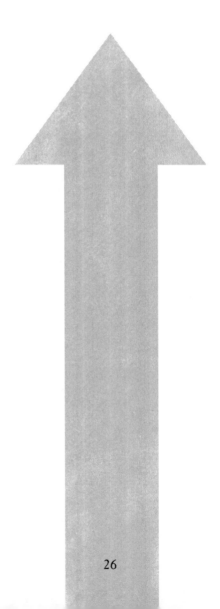

Chapter Three:
CONFIDENCE

People frequently ask me, "How do you do what you do?" "How can you stand up in an OR all day doing a single case?" "How can you stand the sight of blood?" "How did you decide to look up noses?" Sometimes the questions are even simpler: "Do you get thirsty or hungry while you're operating?" "Don't you have to use the bathroom during a long case?" All good questions.

The most interesting question is: "How do you function in an emergency situation?" When I was a beginner in medicine, this question meant, "Will I be able to function in an emergency situation? Will I panic? Will I make the right calls? Will I save the patient's life (and what if I don't)?" Following are my thoughts on these questions.

One Wednesday evening in my second year of residency, after a full day of operating in the morning and seeing patients in the clinic in the afternoon, we had to help an attending do a revision tracheotomy. The patient was an obese man with a history of obstructive sleep apnea (OSA)—a condition in which the airway closes off at night, causing inability to breathe. This results in inefficient sleep and daytime fatigue, and in severe cases can lead to heart disease, lung disease, stroke, and even sudden death. This patient hadn't responded to the typical nonsurgical treatments for sleep apnea and was unable to tolerate CPAP (continuous positive airway pressure), an excellent treatment for OSA that involves sleeping with a mask that is connected to a small machine. That machine generates pressure to hold open the airway.

The patient had to have a tracheotomy—an opening in the neck into the trachea through which a small tube is placed. This tracheostomy tube could be plugged during the day to allow the patient to eat, speak, and breathe normally, but at night it's unplugged so air can flow directly into the trachea. The patient was also schizophrenic. He did well for a while after his first tracheotomy, but during a relapse of his mental illness, removed his tracheostomy tube. (*Tracheotomy* is the procedure. *Tracheostomy* is the resultant opening.) Tracheostomy openings can close within hours after a tube is removed. This patient had an initial tracheotomy, then two more revision (or repeat) tracheotomies because he'd removed the tubes himself.

He'd presented to the emergency room with difficulty breathing. Despite multiple attempts to improve his breathing, his airway acutely obstructed Wednesday morning, and he was unable to breathe. A general surgeon proceeded with a cricothyroidectomy (a temporizing technique much faster than a tracheotomy) to establish the patient's airway, and a temporary breathing tube was placed, restoring normal oxygen levels. This surgeon saved his life. A few hours later we were asked to set this patient up for a revision tracheotomy since he needed a more stable artificial airway in order to go home. The patient was added to the operating room schedule at the end of the day.

That brings us to Wednesday night. The attending surgeon, the chief resident, and I were ready to proceed with the tracheotomy. The patient weighed about 350 pounds and had a very short, stout neck with a tremendous amount of scarring over the trachea. One concern in doing a tracheotomy is that, in some cases, the large vessels that come off the heart and extend up under the sternum (breast bone) can occasionally be so high that they are in the lower neck, in the region of the trachea where the tracheostomy tube will be placed. Also, in someone with a lot of scar tissue and prior surgeries in this area, there is a chance that the scar tissue will have pulled the arteries and veins up into the surgical field, and the vessels may be hard to see within the scar. The biggest artery in question is the innominate artery (translated "no-name artery"). If cut, this artery bleeds profusely. Imagine cutting a hole in a hose when the water is turned on full strength. You can hear the water squirting out. When this vessel is cut, you get "audible bleeding" and the patient can exsanguinate (bleed out).

Within minutes of making the skin incision, the main surgeon identified that the trachea was fairly low in the neck and the area where the tracheostomy should be placed was just above the sternum. The entire surgical field suddenly and rapidly filled with blood. It gushed so rapidly from the wound that it flowed back into the throat through the cricothyroidotomy incision, then came out through the bronchoscope and up through the anesthesia tubing into the anesthesia machine. There was blood everywhere. The patient's heart continued to beat (now rapidly) but his blood pressure dropped to nothing. It was clear he would die within minutes. We all tried to hold pressure on the bleeding site, hoping a thoracic or vascular surgeon was in the hospital. But the bleeding vessel retracted under the sternum, so we couldn't compress the vessel and control the bleeding. His chest needed to be opened for access to the injured vessel.

We "STAT" (medical term for "immediate") paged the cardiothoracic team and asked the nurses to get the equipment needed for opening the chest. The intern on the cardiothoracic team started to extend the skin incision from the neck down to the bottom of the sternum. Then she stopped and said she'd done this only in the lab and was nervous about proceeding. At this point, I followed an important rule I'd taught myself: "In an emergency medical situation, the only one who has any right to panic is the patient." I turned to the scrub nurse and said, "Give me the saw." I placed the sternal saw under the top of the sternum, lifted the saw so I didn't risk cutting through any major structures under the sternum, and cut the sternum in half from top to bottom. I then placed the large chest retractor, opened it, and identified the bleeding site in the vessel. This allowed us to hold pressure and begin to reduce the blood loss, and the anesthesia team re-established a blood pressure.

The vascular team arrived, scrubbed in, and stitched the vessel. While they did this, I placed two large-bore intravenous catheters, one into each femoral vein, to give the patient fluids—including blood—more rapidly. Once the blood vessel was repaired, the tracheostomy was created as planned. We saved the patient. He recovered with only a mild stroke postoperatively that did not cause any permanent neurologic problems.

Confidence Under Stress

What makes us perform well in a stressful or emergency situation? What allows us to do the right thing when seconds count? Confidence: confidence in our abilities, our knowledge, and our thought processes. Confidence to take prior experiences and apply them, even in new situations. I had never opened a chest—and have not opened one since. My father is a carpenter, so I've used jig saws and table saws and hand saws, but I'd never used a sternal saw. The only time I'd seen a patient's chest opened was when the chief of surgery used a bone-cutting knife (not a saw) to cut the sternum to explore for a parathyroid tumor.

> *Our talents, abilities, and knowledge are at our beck and call.*

I opened this patient's chest because he would have died before a chest surgeon got there. "Doing the right thing" meant saving this man's life at all costs.

Anatomy was one of my strongest areas in medical school. As I placed the saw under this patient's sternum to split it open, pages of anatomy books flashed through my head, telling me how close I was to the vital structures underneath. I also had confidence in my dexterity.

My point is that our talents, abilities, and knowledge are at our beck and call. Confidence is recognizing and trusting these and applying them appropriately. When we access these abilities to help ourselves, to help others, and to make the world a better place, we do the right thing.

Positive Anxiety

We do a lot of tonsillectomies in an ear, nose, and throat practice. Post-tonsillectomy bleed occurs in 1-2% of patients undergoing tonsillectomy, typically between seven and 10 days after tonsillectomy, when scabs come off the areas where the tonsils were removed. Most bleeds occur in the middle of the night. The bleeding blood vessel is usually very small, but it bleeds profusely. As it's in the patient's throat (and therefore the airway), it's frightening for the patient and family. It's not uncommon to see the following message on my beeper at 2 a.m.: "Johnny So-and-So, four-year-old patient of Dr. XYZ, had tonsillectomy seven days ago, bleeding profusely, on way to hospital."

What's going through my mind as I drive to the hospital? Adrenaline is causing my heart to race. I'm driving fast—this child is depending on me—and I'm thinking: What if the child is losing a lot of blood? What if his airway is an issue? What if I can't stop the bleeding easily? Then I begin to think worst-case scenarios. In rare cases, the bleeding is from one of the larger vessels. One in 3,000 tonsillectomy cases requires a neck incision to get access to one of these vessels to tie it off. (Usually tonsil bleeding is controlled through the mouth, the same way we remove the tonsils.)

Where does confidence fit in? I've been in this situation numerous times so I draw on my experience. Rarely have I had to open the neck, and I know how to manage the airway if there's a problem. I run through the options for controlling the bleeding. I consider the type of suture I'll use and the technique of placing it. I've done these techniques numerous times. I consider the possibility of opening the neck. I think about the times I've had to do this, and I run through the anatomy.

In other words, I use anxiety in a healthy way to organize my thoughts. I'm able to do this because I'm confident in my abilities. I walk into this situation knowing I can stop the bleeding. I remind myself that panicking does not work.

Confidence, not Cockiness

I know my limitations. When I'm driving into that emergency tonsil bleed, I also consider what to do if I can't stop the bleeding. So I also plan for failure. This is not negative thinking. It is realistic thinking. Foremost in my mind is the idea of teamwork. If the airway is an issue, I'll need anesthesia to work quickly with me to establish a safe airway and prevent the patient from breathing in (aspirating) blood. If the patient's neck needs to be opened I need the nursing staff to quickly get the necessary equipment. I may need another ENT surgeon to do an invasive radiologic procedure called embolization.

Being willing to call for help differentiates confidence from foolish pride or cockiness. Recognizing our limitations and knowing when to call for help are traits of the truly confident. At the end of the movie Magnum Force, Clint Eastwood's Harry Callahan says, "A man's got to know his limitations." In our field, the surgeon who oversteps his bounds, or who delves into areas beyond his capabilities, is a "cowboy" and potentially a danger to the patient. It's good to have pride in our work; it's bad to let pride dictate our work.

Many patients want a second opinion about a diagnosis or a treatment plan, especially with respect to surgery. Maybe they have a personality conflict with the physician. Maybe they want to go to a facility that specializes in the condition. Often patients want a second opinion just to make sure that surgery is the right thing to do. I welcome this. In fact, I often give patients names of knowledgeable surgeons. After all, my goal is that patients get better. I want to do the right thing for my patients.

Applying Confidence

Let's translate these ideas into non-medical applications. We derive confidence from our knowledge base, so try learn as much as possible in our areas of interest, whether career or hobby. Then trust that you'll be willing to use and present that knowledge. Also, be willing to make a mistake. If we don't try, we cannot succeed.

Suppose you are in a corporate meeting and your CEO is looking for an idea to boost the company's presence in the marketplace. You've had vast marketing experience but are new to the company, so want to hold back. You've begun to form some marketing ideas. This is an opportunity to present them. You don't have to give a detailed presentation. Just know that if your ideas are questioned, you have answers. People may disagree with you. But they will recognize your confidence in stepping up to the plate.

Making the Right Mistakes

Part of being confident is being willing to make mistakes. We wouldn't make progress if we didn't try new things. Have a contingency plan. If a patient is bleeding in the middle of the night, I'll use the most standard treatments. If my procedure fails, I need to be able to think ahead to my next move. It's a grave error to try to fix a problem by mounting mistake upon mistake. In medicine, we speak about *Primum non nocere*—"First, do no harm." We have to be willing to try new things and possibly make mistakes, but we need to have a Plan B waiting in the wings. When we do not, we can compound mistake upon mistake and lose sight of the big picture.

During my medical school rotation in the surgical ICU (intensive care unit), a surgical resident was having a particularly hard time. No matter what he did, it was never right in the attending surgeon's eyes. A patient with a severe abdominal infection had developed a lot of fluid in the abdomen and was having significant metabolic problems. The resident tried to reduce the patient's fluid volume by giving him diuretics. The problem was that the fluid was not sitting in the circulatory system on which the diuretics work, but in the abdomen. The patient was already losing fluid from the blood vessels of the circulatory system into his abdomen.

When the resident gave the diuretics, the fluid that was excreted came from the patient's circulatory system, not the abdominal fluid. The patient's heart rate went up, blood pressure decreased, and the patient went into a low circulating volume state (hypovolemia), heading into shock. The nurses pointed this out, but the resident became obstinate. Instead of listening and reassessing, he continued his plan, compounding the error throughout the night. Fortunately, surgeons make rounds early. The attendings assessed the situation, took corrective action, and the patient did well. The resident and the medical students (because we took overnight call and were chastised along with the residents if something went wrong) were strongly and publicly taken to task for the poor management of this patient. The resident was not wrong for making the initial error, but for not recognizing it was an error that should not have been repeated over and over.

Overconfidence and Insecurity

Overconfidence can come from a failure to recognize our limitations. People who are overconfident can be as dangerous, or more dangerous, than those without ability or knowledge. In the overconfident, pride may stand in the way of asking for help.

Overconfidence can be a sign of insecurity. In medical school on rounds, there were some very smart people who studied hard, knew the answers, and were confident. They also admitted it when they didn't know something. The insecure people, however, tried to "one-up" everyone. They'd sneak a peek at their copies of the Washington Manual or other medical pocket texts to be first with the correct answer. When someone else was first, they'd say, "I was going to say that." Typically, they were easily exposed. They couldn't expound on the topic or apply the knowledge to clinical situations. They were more interested in impressing the attendings than learning the information. They'd try to withhold information about patients from the other students and residents so they could be first to present it on rounds. They'd take care of the chief of surgery's patient to impress the chief, but neglect other patients and miss many learning experiences. They see your success as an affront. They want to succeed, but only at the cost of your failure.

If I take pleasure in a colleague's failure, I show incredible insecurity and a lack of compassion. When a colleague fails it likely means a patient had a bad outcome, a surgeon's confidence was shaken, and a hospital's reputation was diminished. How can I take pleasure in that?

When we are confident, we're happy to see others do well.

This behavior isn't limited to medicine. In the corporate world, management asks you and your associates to come up with ways to reduce spending by 10%. You come up with ideas and share them with each other. Some insecure co-workers try to shine over everyone else. They steal your ideas or take credit for them. But how bad will they look in front of the CEO when they stop dead in their tracks, unable to present the next steps? Insecure people are eventually exposed.

Sometimes insecure people get ahead, and you have to answer to them. You may not get credit for your ideas. If your insecure superior constantly holds you back, you may need to confront her. If that doesn't work, you may need to seize an opportunity to present an idea directly to your CEO, or find an organization that can better use your talents. Don't let others undermine your confidence. In fact, use such opportunities to build your confidence.

Too many insecure people get caught up in the "zero-sum game." They believe there is one pie, and if they're to get a bigger slice, everyone else has to get a smaller one. When we are confident, we're happy to see others do well.

I am not a fan of schadenfreude—taking pleasure in another person's failure or misery. Another person's failure does not make my life better. I have to do the best that I can. If I'm confident in my abilities, it doesn't matter if others around me are also doing well. In fact, better for the patients, for the practice, for the hospital, and for the community.

I'm sure we've all felt schadenfreude. Here's an example. I'm from Boston, so let's say the Yankees have beaten the Red Sox to win the American League Pennant. I'm upset and disappointed. The Yankees' fans are happy and take some pleasure in the Red Sox fans' loss, but they're also happy that the Yankees are going to the World Series. As a baseball fan, I watch the World Series. For the sake of argument, say the Yankees lose. Suppose I'm ecstatic that the Yankees lost and I enjoy seeing their fans' disappointment. That, my friends, is schadenfreude.

Have the confidence to use your knowledge and abilities, particularly to help others. My father started out as a carpenter, worked for large commercial companies, and gradually became a superintendent, then a project manager, and eventually a senior vice president for a large construction firm. He never went to college. He had a hard life (his father died one month before he was born), yet I've watched him run meetings with engineers and architects and have seen them ask him for advice. I've watched him redraw blueprints because the theoretical concerns that the blueprints addressed did not apply to the practical situation. My father is confident doing these things because he draws on years of experience and construction knowledge. This is confidence. (Yes, I am very proud of him!) Confidence means balancing ability and humility, and recognizing our knowledge and our limitations. When we are confident we can make the greatest impact on those around us; we can affect the greatest change, make the biggest difference, and do the right thing.

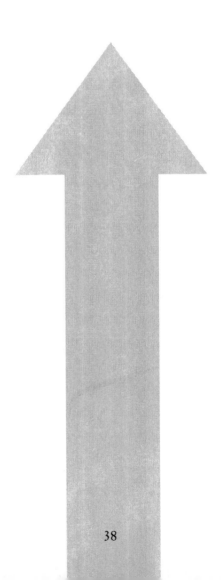

Chapter Four:
CONTRIBUTIONS TO SOCIETY

What will my contribution to society be? What will yours be? Do we need to make one? My main driving force in becoming a physician was wanting to help people. Part of being human and a member of society is using our abilities to contribute to society and make the world a better place. That is our obligation.

There's great satisfaction in helping others. The following examples aren't intended to "toot my own horn," but to show that we all have many opportunities to share our talents, and that someone will always appreciate that sharing.

The staff, administrators, and doctors at Lowell General Hospital set up a multidisciplinary head and neck cancer clinic at our local cancer center to save patients from driving 30-to-45 minutes to the larger academic centers in Boston. Patients may have complex procedures done in Boston, but can have their follow-up appointments locally. This removes a huge burden. A financial consultant would probably say the time spent at the cancer center is a "money loser" and I could "do better" seeing patients in my own office. But I'm contributing to the community, and that's more important to me.

Part of my commitment to treating patients with head and neck cancer is trying to prevent the disease. My daughter's high school asked me if I would speak to the students about the risks of tobacco use. I give this lecture twice a year. Midway through the lecture, I show a picture of myself in the 1980s playing guitar in clubs, then play for about five minutes, just shredding away on my guitar through a little amplifier.

I do this to show the kids that I was a kid once (in the Stone Age, I believe, but nevertheless still a kid) and that I understand peer pressure and "being cool" and taking risks. This is an opportunity to reach hundreds of kids and I hope decrease their use of tobacco products and the related risks of cancer, heart disease, lung disease, and stroke. It's very gratifying to give this lecture (particularly since I get some compliments on my guitar playing. I think the kids are usually shocked that there's some old guy on stage playing Eddie Van Halen solos!).

My dad has engineering and architectural students rotate through his construction job sites to learn about the field. Administrator friends have business students spend time with them to learn the ropes of their careers. Friends in music management take on interns to show them the ins and outs of the music business.

Some of my most meaningful contributions were contributions of time—spending time with cancer societies, or doing things outside my career like coaching soccer, or through a school reading program, reading one of my favorite books to a class. Opportunities to contribute outside our careers or fields of interest are often the simplest and yet most gratifying, and often the most appreciated.

When I was a kid, we were lucky to have a public school system in Medford, Mass., where we could play violin, viola, cello, and/or bass, from second grade through high school. We played in orchestras and performed a few times a year in town. We even had summer programs. I wanted to give something back to kids who are interested in music, particularly kids who can't afford their own instruments.

Do the Right Thing

I searched for a local charity that helped underprivileged kids get involved in music. My friend Keith introduced me to the Music and Youth Initiative (www.musicandyouth.org). I donated guitars and equipment, and set up some YouTube videos of my playing to try to direct attention to this charity. You can see me on my YouTube channel ENTShred. Tom Hamilton from Aerosmith is very involved in this charity. Though I wasn't giving back to the community that helped me get my musical education, I was paying it forward, so to speak, by contributing to a musical program where the kids can really use the support.

My point is that most of us feel a sense of obligation to contribute to our communities. Maybe this feeling comes from a belief in reciprocity, the idea of "giving back to the community." Maybe the need to contribute comes from wanting to help fulfill the promise we see in those around us, particularly our youth, and turn that potential into reality. Maybe we contribute to a cause *Opportunities to contribute outside our careers or fields of interest are often the simplest and yet most gratifying, and often the most appreciated.* because of personal experience. I tend to support organizations that help the ill or underprivileged, because I've seen the hardship caused by diseases like cancer and the difficulties the underprivileged have in getting the chance to tap into their potential.

It feels good to help others. When I heard the kids from the Music and Youth Initiative play those guitars, it was an amazing feeling.

As for money, each small contribution can go a long way. I looked up Project Mosquito Net and learned that every 30 seconds a child dies of malaria. Ten dollars can buy a long-lasting net that can prevent such a death. Ten dollars!

We all can make contributions that seem inconsequential but that can create the framework for a major global effort. We who live in climates with a lot of snow (I live in New England) can attest to the fact that all those little, *inconsequential* snowflakes quickly add up to a huge blizzard when they all decide to fall at the same time.

Societal Footprint

Our "carbon footprint" is a concern for global warming. We want to keep it small. So I propose the following term (I apologize if it's been used): "The Societal Footprint." I was going to call this the "Social Footprint," but that sounded like a measure of how much fun you are at parties. The Societal Footprint refers to our impact on society. The bigger the Societal Footprint, the more we have contributed. Mother

Good deeds are infectious.

Teresa—huge Societal Footprint; Martin Luther King, Jr.—huge Societal Footprint; Doctors without Borders—huge Societal Footprint. Arthur Lauretano, M.D.—small Societal Footprint, but trying to get a bigger shoe size. There can be negative Societal Footprints—Ponzi schemes and banking and mortgage disasters, or the oil spills that have damaged our coastlines.

How do we want to be remembered? Recall Dickens' "A Christmas Carol," when Scrooge is in the presence of the Ghost of Christmas Yet to Come. People are celebrating his demise. Think of Tiny Tim's lonely crutch next to the fireplace, a reminder of something Scrooge could have prevented. Then think about Scrooge after his transformation—a second father to Tiny Tim, and a man who knew how to keep Christmas.

We can all be role models for our children, our community, or the nation. If we're in the public eye, we have the power to make an impact on society. If we're athletes or musicians, millions of kids may look up to us, and there are many messages they need to hear: stay in school, stay away from drugs, and make the world a better place.

Any time we can make the world a better place, we are doing the right thing. An insurance commercial on TV shows a person doing a good deed. Someone witnesses it. In the next scene, that person does a good deed. Someone else sees it and goes on to do a good deed. The pattern comes full circle. Good deeds are infectious.

Do No Harm

I've mentioned our saying in medicine—*Primum non nocere*— "First, do no harm." One of my mentors in general surgery, Dr. Silen, used to say something like: If we have to give a second medication to counteract adverse effects from the first medication, then there was probably something wrong with giving the first medication. First, do no harm.

I had a patient with voice box cancer that had spread to the lymph nodes in his neck. He was treated and the cancer was in remission, but came back. The node in the right neck was close to the bone at the base of his skull. If the cancer traveled into the bone, I wouldn't be able to remove all of it, and it would rapidly grow back. He'd already received full course radiation, so we couldn't give more. Our only chance to cure him was to remove all the cancer. The surgery required removing his voice box and all lymph nodes in the neck. If the lymph node at the skull base was invading into the skull and not removable, we'd be able to give him only palliative treatment with chemotherapy to slow the tumor growth to prolong his life and keep him comfortable. Were this the case, it wouldn't make sense to remove his voice box, since he would likely die within months from the cancer. Therefore, we decided to dissect the neck first, assess the base of skull, and remove the voice box only if I could first remove all the cancer in the neck. The tumor was invading the skull base, so we closed up without removing the voice box. He passed away a few months later, but could speak to his family up until the end.

Removing his voice box would have made his last few months miserable. You may have heard the expression, "The surgery was a success but the patient died." Even if the procedure goes well, we must ensure we do no permanent harm. A "successful" leg amputation does harm if it's the wrong leg. This is why we do a "timeout" in the OR. Before we start the surgery, the circulating nurse reads the patient's name, birth date, procedure planned (including side and site of the body), medications given, and medications on the surgical field.

How does this apply to daily life? If an oil executive looked at an oil well and thought, "First, I need to ensure this oil well does no harm," safety checks would be done and corners wouldn't be cut. The same amount of vigilance should be applied elsewhere.

Do no harm. Try to improve society. Act locally, think globally. Try to leave a Societal Footprint you can be proud of. Be a role model. Small contributions make a difference. The late Marc Bolan (from the band T. Rex) said, "Be strong and follow your own convictions. You can't assume there's a lot of time to do what you like."

One contribution can make a huge difference and have a huge impact on society. When we contribute our time and devote our talents, abilities, and resources to help others, we make the world a better place and that's doing the right thing.

Chapter Five:
PREJUDICE

Prejudice has no place in my life—no place at all. My nationality, and most others, have positive and negative stereotypes. I'm an Italian-American and proud of it. Members of my family have been subjected to prejudice because they're of Italian descent. Most nationalities have suffered this. The human propensity for prejudice is ancient. Why do we tolerate it? Why is it acceptable to see someone as inferior?

What do I want you to see when you see me? I want you to see me as I am, Arthur Lauretano, M.D., a dedicated, extremely compulsive individual who is a surgeon, a family man, and I hope a good person who wants to take care of people regardless of walk of life, race, color, or creed. If you want to say I'm short in stature, a bit overweight (I'm working on it), Italian-American, fine, but those are immaterial. My character and commitment to others is what I want you to see.

> *Our interactions should not be influenced by ethnicity, skin color, gender, or religious beliefs.*

Our interactions should not be influenced by ethnicity, skin color, gender, or religious beliefs. If that can work in the small microcosm of my surgeon's office, wouldn't it be great if we could apply that on a larger scale! The great Martin Luther

King, Jr. stated, "I have a dream that my four little children will one day live in a nation where they will not be judged by the color of their skin but by the content of their character."

How does this fit into my "A Surgeon's Approach to Life" mentality? There is no room for prejudice when you're a physician of any type. Here's a true story.

Learning from AIDS

When I was working at an academic institution in Boston in the early 1990s, I treated a large number of patients with AIDS. One told me that my name frequently came up at his support group because the community felt I was among the few ENT surgeons who would operate on patients with AIDS. Many patients got terrible opportunistic infections (infections with unusual organisms that affect people with compromised immune systems) in their sinuses. They required a combination of sinus surgery and fairly toxic antibiotic regimens. Some over time looked even sicker than my end-stage cancer patients. One patient went blind from opportunistic infections in both eyes, then developed severe pulmonary infections and Kaposi's Sarcoma. Many died.

Most AIDS patients at the city hospital where I worked during medical school had contracted their disease from intravenous drug abuse. Across town at a different institution, most of my AIDS patients were homosexual males. Did it matter? From a disease standpoint, back then, we wondered whether the two populations had different strains of the virus. It didn't matter to me how these patients contracted AIDS. It mattered that I gave them the same compassion all my patients deserve.

The prejudice and hostility these patients suffered reminded me of what I've read of the Black Death or leprosy—the belief that

AIDS was a curse on behavior—sexual behavior, substance abuse, and so on. When we began to understand the disease, and large populations of people with AIDS were identified in Africa and Haiti, racial prejudice entered the mix.

Ethnicity

There are times in medicine where ethnicity matters. Some diseases affect one ethnic group or one geographic area more than another. When I see a person of Mediterranean descent with anemia, I'll consider thalassemia. If an African-American patient has postoperative multiple organ system failure, I'll consider sickle cell anemia. If a patient who grew up in Africa and recently moved to the U.S. has severe shaking chills (rigors), I'll consider malaria. A French-Canadian patient with a swallowing disorder and drooping eyelids may have oculopharyngeal dystrophy. A patient from China with fluid in the ears and a mass in the nasopharynx (back of the nose) may have nasopharyngeal carcinoma. A child of Eastern European Jewish descent with mental developmental delays, convulsions, or blindness may have Tay-Sachs disease.

I love learning about my patients' cultures. In Lowell, Mass., where I practice medicine now, we have a large populations of French, Portuguese, Brazilians, Hispanics, Irish, Greeks, Cambodians, Vietnamese, Laotians, Thai, Burmese, Indians, and Italians (sorry if I missed any). We are seeing more immigrants from Africa.

Culture

I also need to be sensitive to cultural differences that may influence treatment, particularly the patient's compliance with a treatment plan. A local large insurer requires a cultural training session just for these issues. For instance, we're very careful about patient privacy, particularly in compliance with HIPAA (the Health Insurance Portability and Accountability Act passed by Congress in 1996), but we need to realize that some ethnic groups expect family members to be part of the decision process. The insurer cites the example of an Asian family that expected children to be included in the decision process. Respecting another person's culture is a key factor in a good patient-doctor relationship. So why can't this apply to all our relationships?

Cultural differences can involve language. When I began to treat Cambodian patients with cancer, I learned it was hard to describe cancer in the Khmer language. One family member said they described it as "The Bad Thing." This can create a greater challenge than explaining, through a translator, a major cancer surgery such as a partial tongue resection and neck dissection (removal of the lymph nodes in the neck and part of the tongue).

Many patients who've just moved here from Africa see appointment times as approximations, not as exact times. Some have shown up an hour late. My approach? I see them. First, it's not unusual for me to run an hour behind. Second, the patient is here, and may have something really bad, like cancer, that I need to treat. If these patients are willing to wait, I'll see them. They never complain about waiting. They're grateful to be seen, they comply with the treatment plan, and they come back for scheduled follow-ups—usually late again!

Religion

Practicing medicine means respecting patients' religious beliefs. A month after the 9/11 attacks and the unfortunate backlash against Muslims, I saw a new patient. He was a very nice young man in his

30s with a large neck mass close to some of the nerves that move the tongue. His thick beard had covered the mass when it was small. A biopsy showed the mass was a benign tumor that would need to be removed because of malignant potential. Surgery would entail shaving his beard and might result in some temporary paralysis in his tongue nerves. My patient wanted to put off treatment until after the religious month. I agreed. He did well and had no problems with tongue motion or sensation.

I saw a patient with a maxillary (cheek) sinus cancer who required surgery. This tends to be a relatively bloody operation, particularly when the tumor is in the back of the sinus and close to a large group (plexus) of veins, as in this case. This patient was 75 years old, so her heart might not withstand a lot of blood loss, which decreases oxygen delivery to the heart and increases the work of the heart. In such procedures it's common to transfuse some units of blood back into the patient. But this patient was a Jehovah's Witness and could not receive blood products. A relative who'd needed a tonsillectomy had been turned down by several surgeons because the risk of delayed bleeding can require repeat surgery and, on rare occasions, a blood transfusion. My patient sought me out because I'd been willing to perform that tonsillectomy. I operated on her because I needed to cure her cancer. But I also needed to respect her wishes. As we started to lose blood, one of my residents walked out because he didn't agree with my decision to operate and not transfuse. I realized the potential risks. If she had needed blood and I refused to provide it, hospital lawyers could have become involved. But we got her through and she lived to an old age, free of cancer.

Gender

The medical field has had gender barriers, but began to destroy them early on. My medical school had the vision to accept a large number of female students and I know many women in medicine whose talents are superlative. Consider the number of women who are great world leaders. Yet we still hear about discrimination in the corporate world and unthinkable crimes and punishments against women.

> *Prejudice disguised as principle, religious passion, nationalism, or moral righteousness is still prejudice.*

In an episode of *American Dad*, Stan (the main character) meets a man who seems the perfect friend, until he learns his friend is an atheist. I asked, Who would I rather be friends with, a good person, who respects others but happens to be an atheist, or a person whose religious convictions have led to prejudice or violence? Prejudice disguised as principle, religious passion, nationalism, or moral righteousness is still prejudice.

Economics

Prejudice based on financial/economic status occurs in the U.S., and is even more rampant in other countries. Patients on welfare make up 15-to-25% of my practice. Some families (of all ethnicities) are particularly large, and all family members are on welfare. If population growth occurs mainly in the poorest socioeconomic group, will this group become a majority but a financial minority?

Medicine is a unique situation. If you come into my office for a neck tumor, I'll take your history, examine you, probably proceed with a needle biopsy of the mass, set you up for diagnostic tests (a CT scan or PET scan or MRI) and, depending on the mass, proceed with surgery or set you up for chemotherapy and radiation therapy. Does your insurance matter to me? Not from a treatment standpoint. All my patients get the same treatment.

Insurance companies set our rates, which are generally based on Medicare rates. When I figure overhead (salaries, staff health insurance and retirement, office lease, and equipment), excluding my income, some insurances pay us less than it costs to see the patient. In other words, from a business standpoint, we're paying to see the patient. Does that change my treatment? Of course not, because doing the right thing means taking care of that patient. The patient's insurance may dictate whether or not she needs a referral to see me, whether we need a pre-certification to get the scan, and so on, but anything I do is the same, regardless of insurance. My goal is to treat my patient to the best of my ability and to make her well.

Consider this scenario. Three people go to a luxury car dealership with different amounts of money, but each amount is less than the cost of the car. Each person pays what he has and drives off with the same luxury car. This is what occurs in medicine. Why do I mention this?

As time goes on the number of people on welfare and other government programs increases, but the payment for medical services by such programs decreases (or fails to keep up with the cost of living). Some physicians may stop accepting patients with these insurances, not because of greed, but because their salaries and overhead increase annually with the cost of living. I know physicians who've stopped taking welfare patients. If more people (including children) rely on government programs to cover their medical care, and if more doctors stop accepting these patients, they will have limited access to local care. They may need to travel miles to academic centers in major cities. Some patients cannot make the travel arrangements. We need to be alert to insidious prejudice.

In an era of political correctness, let's make sure we don't infringe on each other's rights. At the same let's not stifle those aspects of our cultures that make our society great. We don't want a homogenized society, at least in my opinion. We want to maintain the unique qualities that make our culture great! When we respect each other's cultures, work to help each other, and engage to form a cohesive community, we're striving to do the right thing.

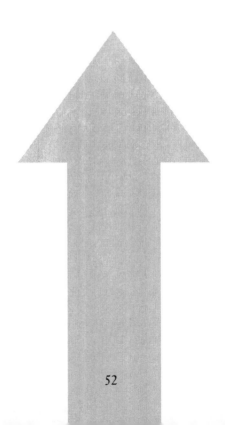

Chapter Six:
FINANCES AND FAIRNESS

I'm in a strange business. I make money when people are sick. A lot of jobs depend on others being at some type of disadvantage. I've paid a lot of money to plumbers because of leaks and clogs and to mechanics because my car wouldn't start. But it's different when you make your income from people being sick. The positive view is that I make my income by making sick people better, and, of course, that's how I look at it. The problem with me is, I hate the financial aspect of my job.

My vision was that I would finish medical school two years early, go to a good ENT residency, then go into an academic practice where I could teach and do complicated cases (I did spend three-and-a-half years in an academic practice). I'd envisioned making a good income. I pictured that, in my 40s, I'd have paid off my house. I'd financially take care of my parents and my wife and kids, and go to work each day not worrying about the bottom line. I'd focus on providing care to inner-city patients with the most complicated head and neck problems, especially those with cancer, regardless of whether they could pay.

Reality was different. Various illnesses in my family left me torn between long hours at work and trying to help out at home. My wife was basically a single mother because I was barely home during my academic practice years. So I decided to work in a private practice in a community closer to home. I was still able to teach, but much less than I'd hoped. Fortunately, I was able to take care of head and neck cancer patients in the community and help set up a head and neck cancer center at Lowell General Hospital. Not a big academic position, but a contribution to the community, which is important to me.

Many of my family's medical problems required money out of pocket because the expenses exceeded insurance coverage. Sometimes these problems required me to take time off from work, resulting in some loss of income. Thank God I had enough not to struggle. It pains me greatly to see my patients, many blue-collar workers, struggle to pay for care and/or lose wages due to illness.

My dream of having a practice based solely on taking care of people and not worrying whether they paid me was slipping away. Many times I don't charge for visits, and until recently, my position at the head and neck clinic was unpaid. But over time I've felt an incredible tug of war between practicing the type of medicine I'd dreamed of and managing financial issues at work and home.

I find it unfortunate that medicine is a business. Rising healthcare costs and increased health insurance premiums and patient co-pays strain an already taxed system. Providers have much less control over fees than most people realize. Reimbursements are based on rates set by Medicare, and billing regulations are very strict.

Why am I telling you this? When a patient who is holding down two jobs to pay for health insurance for his family comes into my office two or three days in a row with his sick kid, he may have to pay a $50 co-pay for each visit. I can't write it off—that co-pay is a contractual agreement between the patient and the insurance company. Collecting it is an agreement I have with the insurance company and also is in compliance with government regulations. So I have to charge him. Some patients cancel appointments because of the co-pay. I refuse to let that happen, so when legally allowable, I care for the patient without any charge. This includes surgical procedures (a recent eight-hour laryngeal cancer surgery comes to mind). But this is terrible business sense, and even if I don't charge patients, if things go wrong, even if I'm not negligent, they could still sue me. So why not be a better business person? Because I care about these patients.

Am I just venting? No; I've learned lessons from looking at the financial aspects of medicine, and from my personal experiences and mistakes. These lessons apply to all of us, no matter what we do for a living. So I'll pass them on to you.

Live Within Your Means

My first point of advice in this chapter is live within your means. In fact, live a bit below your means. My house is nothing extravagant, but I still have a fat, juicy mortgage. My car is eight years old and has 140,000 miles on it. I didn't expect physician reimbursements to go down, or the costs of doing business to rise so much, and I didn't expect to feel the financial pressures connected with caring for the most needy.

Periodically, I consider whether I should continue to take certain insurances that reimburse poorly, but I'm reluctant to drop any of them because I don't want to limit access to care. If my bottom line is so tenuous that I have to deny someone care due to financial reasons, then I am living above my means. Living within or a bit below our means provides reserve for tough times and may relieve some stress.

Living within or a bit below our means provides reserve for tough times and may relieve some stress.

In financial issues, we often talk about what is fair. A professional negotiator once told me that *fair* is the real "F-word." We've all heard someone say that it is not fair that someone else makes more money or has more possessions. Let's look at this in terms of money, medicine, and prestige.

In medicine, we may discuss models for dividing practice income among the members of a physician group. There is always a debate. Some models divide income evenly among the members, even if the volume of patients seen by each is not equal. Others divide it unequally and base it on severity of cases, or numbers of patients each sees, or some other method. There is no best way, and each practice may choose a different model. In each case, there may

> *Fairness is complicated because it's all relative. It depends on our vantage point.*

be those who see it as fair and those who do not. Some may make more money, or some may work less for the same share of the money. It takes a bigger person to realize that we may have to make some sacrifices to support our colleagues. We must choose a model that supports the greater good, not just our own interests.

Fairness is a difficult concept. We may instinctively know what's fair, yet putting it into practice is difficult. Fairness varies with vantage point. Let's say we define fairness as what serves the greater good. We'll use this a springboard to a deeper discussion of fairness.

When President Obama signed his health care plan into law, many felt providing health care to everyone was fair. But when the details were ironed out, some found their own coverage had to change so that more people could be covered. For the benefit of the greater good, they had to make some sacrifices. Some of these people, who initially supported Obamacare, now wanted it repealed. Fairness is all relative.

A poster designed for the workplace in the early 1970s went something like this:

> The parts of the body were having a debate about who should be the boss of the body. The heart felt he should be the boss because as soon as the heart stops, the body dies. The brain wanted to be the boss since it felt that, by nature, she was the one who called all the shots. The stomach put in its claim, citing the fact that it processed food for energy for the body. The musculoskeletal system, the kidneys, and the liver all staked a claim. And then the anus spoke up. Before the anus could even present a plausible argument, the rest of the body parts began to laugh uncontrollably. "Are you kidding? You don't do anything, how could you be the boss!" At this, the anus became quiet and closed up. It stayed like this for days, and gradually, the body became increasingly constipated. The stomach couldn't function, the brain couldn't think straight, the heart rhythm became abnormal. Everything began to shut down. Finally, the body parts got together and said, "Enough is enough! Anus, you can be the boss!" The moral of the story is that you don't have to be a brain or have a lot of heart to be the boss, you just have to be an ASS!

This story shows fairness is complicated because it's all relative. It depends on our vantage point.

Fairness is difficult. It can involve money or power or prestige; the better part in the play, or the solo in the band; or the starting position on the team. Speaking cynically, we're all in favor of fairness, as long as it is fair to us. The details make it hard. In fairness (pun intended) to all of us, I think it's human nature to want to protect ourselves and what we believe we deserve.

Being Flexible

If we're *inflexible* in how we view "fairness" we may conclude: "Life is unfair; get used to it." This statement, reportedly from a Bill Gates speech to high-school students, is number one in a list of 11 things the students would not learn in high school. (I was under the impression this quote came from Bill Gates in *Business @ the Speed of Thought: Using a Digital Nervous System*, 1999, Grand Central Publishing, but found a reference to this list as given by Charles Sykes in *Dumbing Down Our Kids*, 1996, St. Martin's Griffin.)

I've seen such inflexibility all too often, and I've seen it cause significant conflict among associates and members of organizations, particularly when dealing with money matters. If I want to call something unfair, I think of these examples (all true stories).

Example 1: A teenager I diagnosed with an aggressive head and neck cancer, despite the best treatment, dies before she has a first date, or goes to the prom.

Example 2: A 29-year-old mother dies suddenly of an aneurysm, leaving three kids behind.

Example 3: Someone caring for a sick loved one gets cancer herself and has to juggle her own appointments with those of her loved one.

We hear such stories too often in the medical fields. They make discussions about fairness based on finances and reimbursement petty and trite.

Before I state my ideas on how to deal with fairness, I want to make something clear. I've read a lot of self-help books and usually found at least one helpful thing in each one. But in some cases I've thought, "It's easy for this author to tell me all this advice because he's already financially set," or some variant of that. In some cases I felt the author was being pretentious. I'm sensitive to this, and I don't want to come off as pretentious or "holier-than-thou." My approach to fairness is something I struggle with every day. I've even re-read this chapter to make sure I'm trying to heed my own advice, because until recently my approach to fairness was to complain when I felt that something was unfair.

Redefine Fairness

My healthier approach is to "redefine fairness." That's it. Each situation puts us in a different position with respect to fairness. When we, as individuals, feel we've been treated unfairly, we need to redefine fairness. As a group, we need to redefine fairness to benefit the greatest number of people. Fairness means providing the greatest good for the greatest number, while minimizing the impact on those who must give something up or make some compromise.

How do I redefine fairness? I've sometimes been the top wager earner and other times near the bottom. I've seen hard-working associates whose compensation didn't seem adequate. When I can, I look for ways to achieve equity. Being fair may mean supporting those on the bottom rung.

If you're a homemaker or a stay-at-home mom or dad, you may think the division of labor is unfair. Your partner who's worked all day wants to come home and relax or go to the gym. But you want help with the chores. When both partners work, the higher earner or the one with longer hours may feel entitled to do less housework. You get the picture.

> *The only person I need to compete with is myself.*

Rather than dwelling on the negative, we can focus on how well the family is doing, or how well you, as part of that family, are doing. That's redefining fairness.

If I redefine what's fair, I simply have to realize I make a good income doing the type of surgery I love to do. I gain a lot in personal growth and experience by being president of the medical staff. You may simply call this the "power of positive thinking," and I don't disagree. We need to leave behind that zero-sum idea, that if I'm doing poorly, it means someone else has a bigger piece of the pie.

So how do I redefine fairness regarding my income? I look only at my own financial numbers; compare them to last year's; and decide whether my income makes sense in light of how many patients I saw, the type of cases I did, and my activities outside the hospital. But I do not look at my associates' numbers.

If I look at this competitively, the only person I need to compete with is myself. I've learned this through practicing martial arts. It doesn't matter if someone gets her black belt before I do, or has a higher rank. My greatest competitor is me. In my practice, I can use prior years' incomes and productivity assessments as benchmarks. If I want to improve my numbers, I can speak to my managing partner, my office manager, and our practice consultant. These are ways to redefine fairness.

Make striving for better mean striving for better than you did in the past, not striving to be better than the guy in the next cubicle or the woman in the office down the hall. So you didn't make the varsity soccer team your first year; keep trying while on the junior varsity.

Do it Anyway

Does redefining fairness always work? Of course not. I've seen patients go through surgery, then chemotherapy, then radiation therapy, and it appears they have beaten their disease, but then six months later, the disease comes back. They go through more chemotherapy and more surgery, but a few months later, the cancer arises in another part of the body, a distant *metastasis*. We treat the metastasis, and it shrinks, then begins to resist treatment, so we opt for stronger treatment, which has more side effects—more hair loss, fatigue, low blood counts that risk infection and require more time in the hospital, nausea, vomiting and weight loss. Finally, a chest radiograph shows the lungs are filled with cancer, and we realize we cannot win. The patients become increasingly fatigued and less responsive as the body's metabolism falters from the effects of the cancer cells. Eventually, the patients slip into a coma and pass away. I've asked what's fair about this. Perhaps I can find a little consolation – we gave the patients more years with family – but often I cannot see any fairness in this.

Sometimes, when I feel I'm being treated unfairly, I consider the personal crises others have faced, or think about global disasters. In the grand scheme of things, my situation isn't so bad.

In discussing fairness so far, I've talked mostly about possessions—what we have or don't have, or what we feel we need, whether material possessions or abilities or knowledge or wisdom. Now I ask you to have perspective regarding what you have and what others may not.

Perspective and Relating to Others

Consider these examples. My son had tremendously flat feet—one of the many genetic gifts I've bestowed on him. Initially he had orthotics, but continued to get pain in his feet and muscle strains in his legs, so missed a lot of activities at school. He underwent physical therapy, but the symptoms came back. Eventually, he underwent surgery, one foot at a time, separated by a six-month interval. Each surgery required one week of inactivity, keeping the foot elevated, then one week of non-weight bearing (on crutches), then a few weeks of wearing a boot, followed by a couple of months of physical therapy.

He'd just had his first surgery and finished the two weeks of non-weight bearing activity. My wife and I were concerned about the long-term success of the procedure, how he would do with physical therapy, and when he would need surgery for the other foot. On the day my little guy went back to school with his boot on, someone came up to me in the middle of a busy work day at the hospital and told me how great his son had done playing soccer over the weekend. His kid was playing up a level (playing with older kids),

> *We should try to relate to others and understand their circumstances, and be sensitive to what they may be going through.*

and had been the star of the game, and other coaches were already recruiting this 10-year-old for a more elite team.

Any other day I might have asked him more about his kid. On this day, I was concerned about my son's foot. I had visions of infections of the implant in his foot, or the implant shifting or coming out, or his having pain, or the procedure not working, and other fears I had as a surgeon and as a dad. Finally, I excused myself and walked away.

Maybe I was a little jealous. So I redefined fairness and got past the idea that my child's need for foot surgery was unfair. I redefined fairness by being grateful there was a treatment for his problem, and his problem was so much less severe than some of the disorders and diseases I see in kids his age. The problem I had with this episode was the other person's lack of perspective. He knew my son had just had surgery and had a hard time playing sports because of this. Also, it was obvious that I was busy—in the middle of checking some lab and CT scan data for my next case. In my response I was trying to show happiness for his son, but also trying to convey that I wanted to move on. However, he kept going on and on about his son.

Recently, someone approached me about his son, an athletic boy who may need the same surgery as my son. I gave him some advice and some names. When we discuss the kids, sports, and so on, I'm first going to ask him how his son is doing, and the tone of the discussions that follow will depend on what he says.

We should try to relate to others and understand their circumstances, and be sensitive to what they may be going through.

Here's another example. I love to buy guitars and, in fact, if I buy any more, my wife will throw me and the guitars out onto the street. At the hospital, I went on and on about a new guitar I wanted. I was discussing the price ($2,500) and how it sounded different than my other 10 or so guitars. After the fact, I realized someone in the conversation had fallen on very hard financial times. Her husband had lost his job and I knew this, yet I went on and on about the guitars. I felt terrible afterwards. I showed a complete lack of perspective. I've been more careful since.

I can't begin to imagine how some of my cancer patients and their parents have felt when they heard other parents describe how beautiful their daughters looked at the prom, when my patients missed the prom because they were recovering from chemotherapy or radiation or surgery.

It's hard to define when people go beyond *informing* to the point of *bragging*. But we know when someone is bragging. We have a visceral sense that a line has been crossed.

I give my parents a hard time about their perspective on possessions (material and nonmaterial), and I tend to ridicule their generation (my dad is 77, my mother 75). They worked hard for what they had, and wanted me to do better. Ironically, though, they had little and learned to be happy with that. They and others in their generation tend to define their children's successes and perhaps their own based on possessions. "Look at the job my son has!" "My daughter just bought a new Mercedes." You get the point. Material things are their measures. This may be why my generation grew up with a certain materialism.

I wanted to be a professional guitar player. This was a constant battle with my parents. I always did well in school, so they expected me to go into one of the professions. But I would've been just as happy going to the Berklee College of Music in Boston (still a dream). Eventually, my desire to help others translated into my going to medical school.

I hope my kids do what makes them happy in life. Material possessions are not my measure of their success. If I can help them, great, but it's *their* achievement. If they're not successful (whatever that may mean), does that make me less of a person? No. It's all about perspective, and it gets back to what I said earlier – it's all relative.

Money and Transparency

Sometimes people who think life's unfair because they didn't reach their goals while others did (the zero-sum game again) are tempted to make subtle, perhaps unethical, changes to make more money or gain recognition. Over time, such practices build until they wonder how they fell so far from their moral and ethical ground.

Take a hypothetical example. One of my favorite surgeries is thyroid surgery (thyroidectomy—removal of the thyroid gland for cancer or for enlargement of the gland). One of my most common surgeries is tonsillectomy.

Let's suppose thyroidectomy pays 10 times more than tonsillectomy. Let's also assume I do 10 times more thyroid surgeries a year than tonsillectomies. An ideal situation from a financial standpoint, right? More important, I'm doing surgery I love. Besides, let's say I dislike tonsillectomies and think they're done too often or that the indications need to be stricter.

Now, say I wake up one morning and *tonsillectomy* pays 10 times more. But I continue to do 10 times more thyroidectomies. My income decreases, but I'm not upset because I enjoy doing thyroid surgery. You'd agree I've not been swayed by finances.

Now, let's reverse things. When I learn that tonsillectomies pay more, I start scheduling more of those, and fewer thyroidectomies. I'm now doing 10 times as many tonsillectomies as thyroidectomies. Clearly, I'm being driven by money. You might question me as a physician because my incentives seem to be financial and not medical.

So I base this on business sense. I explain that my overhead is very high and I can't afford a big reduction in income. I'm making a decision based on finances, but I'm being upfront about my reasons. I still contend tonsillectomies should be a last resort, and for very strict indications. My medical principles have not changed.

Now suppose I tell you finances have nothing to do with it. Instead, I explain that the indications for tonsillectomy should be loosened and the indications for thyroidectomy made more strict. I'm not being honest with you or, more important, with myself. This lack of transparency can lead to a slippery slope. We start to make decisions for the wrong reasons, justify them (even to the point of lying to ourselves), and begin to follow patterns of behavior and practices we might never have considered.

Having my price doesn't equate to selling my soul.

A lack of transparency is behind some of the problems we see every day. Suppose you manage a fuel company (oil, coal or gas), and you realize that monthly maintenance checks have increased costs. You're responsible for the bottom line so you decide some checks can be done less often or even overlooked. These decisions increase your bottom line and seem to have no negative effects. So you make a few more cuts, neglect a few more checks. Soon, your section has safety issues. And you've been dishonest with yourself, convincing yourself of the good you're doing for the company.

Then one day, it happens—a major oil spill, or oil rig disaster, or mine collapse, or gas explosion—and suddenly you're responsible for loss of life, environmental devastation, and collapse of the company whose bottom line you so closely managed. We've heard about such incidents and subsequent investigations that reveal safety violations. This wasn't intentional. Recall the public service message once run on TV by the Partnership for a Drug-Free America. It stated, "No one ever says, 'I want to be a junkie when I grow up.'"

Many such behaviors begin with what seems to be a benign cutting of corners, small white lies. But they snowball until dishonesty becomes part of our moral fabric. You've heard the expression "Every man has his price." Well, I have my price. If you offered me my current salary but said I could focus on head and neck cancer surgery without worrying about office overhead or needing to supplement the low reimbursements for cancer surgery by seeing more patients, I'd probably jump at the opportunity. Yes, I have my price, but in this case it would allow me to help people, function within my moral and ethical framework, and do the right thing. Having my price doesn't equate to selling my soul.

Humility vs. Perfection

We are not defined by our abilities and possessions. What matters is what we do with our abilities, especially if we benefit others. The word "humility" comes to mind. If we're humble, we don't need to brag.

A few years ago I read a book titled *Shut Up About Your Perfect Kid: A Survival Guide for Ordinary Parents of Special Children,* by Gina Gallagher and Patricia Konjoian (revised edition published by Three Rivers Press, August 3, 2010). The authors are two sisters who live in our community. On their website (www.shutupabout.com) they describe themselves as "among the growing number of parents raising children with disabilities. . . . fed up with listening to parents brag about their 'perfect children' and never asking about theirs."

> *When we're exactly who we want to be, then we're truly wealthy.*

The sisters decided writing a book would be therapeutic. In 2006, they self-published their first book, *Shut Up About Your*

ARTHUR LAURETANO

Perfect Kid! The Movement of Imperfection, exploring the humorous, heartwarming side of raising an imperfect child in a world preoccupied with perfection. Tracy Anglada (executive director of BPChildren and author of *Intense Minds: Through the Eyes of Young People with Bipolar Disorder*) states, "*Shut Up About Your Perfect Kid* is the perfect antidote to a society obsessed with perfection...Their journey is similar to that of many parents who have been filled with conflicting feelings about their children. But at the end of the day, instead of seeing their children's differences, they see their determination and spirit. It's that determination and spirit that has changed their lives in every way. It's also what they would like the rest of the world to embrace. This book is a breath of fresh air to parents of kids with all sorts of abilities."

This book speaks volumes on the issue of perspective. Our society is obsessed with perfection. We're especially obsessed with having our kids be the best. Taking this further, if my kid is better than yours, I'm better or more successful than you.

It's too easy to dismiss those who aren't perfect. In fact, we often dismiss people because they fail to be the best in the activity or talent that occupies us at a given time. It's problematic that some of us live vicariously through our children's accomplishments. I may be disappointed if my daughter's soccer team loses a tournament, but it doesn't come close to the disappointment I'll feel when a patient's pathology result shows she has cancer. Again, it's all about perspective; it's all relative.

When I consider the finiteness of life, I believe we should approach each day with the perspective that our time on Earth is limited. The things that are *really* important are so much more significant than how much better my car is or how much more exotic your vacations are.

I marvel at people, who in a situation I would find difficult or exasperating, can find the humor, the good, the positive, and the beautiful. Our character—who we are, and what we do for others—is what matters. When we're exactly who we want to be, then we're truly wealthy.

Writing this chapter was cathartic and therapeutic. I've tried to follow the principles I've set forth and at times (sometimes often) have failed miserably. I've vowed to be honest in this book, so I have no problem admitting that many of these ideas are hard to adopt and harder to practice.

I have a long way to go before I've mastered these ideas. So I will read this chapter again and again, particularly when I face a situation that tests these principles. I hope you've found this material thought-provoking. If you find just one helpful idea, then I'm satisfied. When we are honest, make difficult choices related to finances and fairness, and take into account the big picture, we are doing the right thing.

ARTHUR LAURETANO

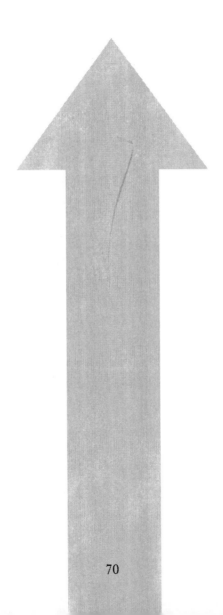

Chapter Seven:
TEAMWORK

Teamwork is an essential part of the surgical care of patients, and an essential part of being a physician. We speak of the surgical team or the medical team or the trauma team or the transplant team or the reconstructive team. Teamwork is also essential to businesses, organizations, households, and to daily life. An example of teamwork in head and neck cancer surgery reflects the dynamics of teamwork in many facets of our daily lives.

Floor-of-mouth cancer is a common head and neck cancer. The floor of the mouth is the soft area under the front of the tongue, behind the lower teeth, where the dentist places the suction. It abuts the lower jaw (the mandible). Many of our patients are in denial about

> *Teamwork is also essential to businesses, organizations, households, and to daily life.*

cancer and, when they develop an ulcer or a lump in the floor of their mouth, they tend to ignore it. If they have poor dentition (bad teeth), they assume such ulcers or lumps are just related to their teeth. So it's not unusual that when a patient comes in with a growth in this part of the head and neck, the cancer is fairly advanced. The cancer may even have eaten into part of the mandible bone, and may have spread into the neck.

When cancer is advanced, patients usually require a combination of surgery (typically done first) and radiation therapy (a few weeks after surgery and usually given over seven weeks). Chemotherapy may also be used to enhance the effect of the radiation therapy. The surgery often involves removing the floor of the mouth, possibly some of the front undersurface of the tongue, part of the jaw bone, and the lymph nodes in the neck. The jaw and floor of the mouth will then require reconstruction to recreate the jaw and allow for speech and swallowing. After sufficient healing, the radiation therapy begins, with or without a radiosensitizing chemotherapy agent. The surgery may sound frightening but the ability to remove a cancer in its entirety is gratifying, especially as so many reconstructive options are available. I love doing these surgeries because I feel I'm helping the patient so much. I used the pronoun "I" in the last sentence, but "we" would be much more appropriate.

First, the patient comes to my office, often referred by the primary care doctor. That provider is an important part of the patient's care throughout treatment. My staff and I evaluate the patient and I identify the growth (we call it a "lion" until we know the pathologic identity). I perform a full examination and then proceed with a fiber optic examination of the patient's throat to make sure there are no other lesions. (Particularly in smokers, there is about a 15% chance of a second cancer.) I biopsy the growth at the patient's first visit and send the specimen to the pathology team.

I discuss the cancer and its treatment with the patient and family, and my staff sets the patient up for CT and PET scans to assess the full extent of the growth. The radiologist reads the scans and confers with me on the findings. Now the team includes the radiologists.

At this point, I see the patient again to go over all the findings. I explain that the biopsy showed cancer, and that the scans show involvement of the bone such that the front part of the jaw needs to be removed. I explain the lymph nodes in the neck need to be removed, but the lungs and rest of the body are free of cancer, so we can cure this cancer with surgery and radiation. I discuss the entire treatment plan, including side effects, complications, survival rates, quality of life, and so on. I arrange for the patient to visit our multidisciplinary head and neck clinic and see the plastic surgeon who will do the reconstruction once I've removed the cancer. All of this surgery will be done in one day.

At the head and neck clinic, the patient sees me and the radiation oncologists (the doctors who give the radiation) and the medical oncologists (who give chemotherapy, if needed). The patient and his family meet the oncology nurses, the social workers, and the technologists who plan and administer the radiation. The patient also meets the nutritionists and the speech and swallowing therapists.

The patient hasn't had surgery yet but the team taking care of him is now huge. Now the patient meets the plastic surgeon, whose team will reconstruct the jaw using a free tissue transfer (a "free flap") that consists of the skin and soft tissue overlying the outside part of the lower leg as well as a piece of bone from that area, the fibula. This fibula free flap is harvested from the patient's leg while I'm working in the mouth and neck to remove the cancer. The free tissue with its blood supply is then tied into the blood supply in the neck so that the tissue can survive. The tissue, along with the bone, is stitched (sutured) in place in the mouth, and the bone is fixed in place with plates and screws.

In preparation for surgery, the patient's primary care doctor reviews all of his medications and other medical problems to make sure the patient is cleared for surgery. The anesthesiologists who put the patient to sleep for the surgery and maintain the patient's airway, ventilation, cardiac function, and so on, meet the patient a few days before surgery and see the patient again in the "holding area" in the operating room, as do I, my team, and the plastics team. The patient meets the surgical residents on my team, the ablative team—the team that removes the cancer—and the residents on the reconstructive plastics team. Many nurses and scrub technicians also participate in the surgery. They meet the patient before the procedure, make sure we all agree as to the part of the body on which we're operating, make sure we have all the equipment we need, and that all consents are signed, labs are checked, and the list goes on. In case we need blood during the surgery, they make sure blood is available.

In the operating room, everyone has a job, and everyone knows it well. We identify the patient, his allergies, the procedure, the medications he has or will receive, and numerous other aspects of our "time out" protocol. Special stockings are placed on the patient's legs to prevent clots in the leg veins. Anesthesia puts the patient to sleep and intubates him (places a breathing tube in the trachea). The nurses put a urinary catheter in place. Anesthesia places an arterial line to monitor blood pressure and draw blood during the surgery. The neck and leg are prepped (cleaned off with a sterilizing solution) and the surgery begins.

Usually at the beginning of such a procedure, we place a tracheostomy tube to replace the initial breathing tube, which is in our way. The surgery produces swelling in the tongue and throat, so the patient needs a stable airway to bypass areas of swelling.

Placing the tracheostomy requires significant communication involving me, my surgical team, and the anesthesia team. Once the tracheostomy tube is placed, I remove the neck nodes and the floor of mouth cancer. At the same time the plastics team operates on the leg to prepare the graft, and we review the surgical defect to decide how much of a graft is needed. Once I remove the tumor, I send pieces of the surrounding normal-appearing membrane to the pathologists, who examine the tissue under the microscope to make sure I've completely removed the cancer (achieved "negative margins"). So the pathologists are involved again while the surgery is in progress. They also process and examine the main tumor specimen that has been removed and analyze the lymph nodes to see how many of them contain cancer.

The plastics team proceeds with putting the jaw back together. That team has its own surgical team, including scrub nurses and technicians to place the graft, stitch it in place, and connect the blood supply. Bone is being transferred, so a representative from the surgical equipment company that makes the plates that hold the bone in position is present to help select the plates that fit this patient's reconstruction.

The surgery takes about six to eight hours and is successful. The cancer is out, and the patient is ready to go to the recovery room (or PACU, post-anesthesia care unit). Enter a new team—the recovery room nurses. They tend to the patient as he clears the effects of anesthesia from his system. Recovery room care, which is part of what is known as critical care, requires specialized nurses (as did the operating room). The anesthesia team and surgeons are still involved. The patient stays in the recovery room for a couple of hours, then is transferred to a patient floor. In such a large surgery, this is either the intensive care unit (ICU) or an intermediate care unit (one step of acuity below the ICU). Here, additional critical care nurses are involved, sometimes an intensivist (a doctor specializing in critical care) and the ablative and reconstructive surgical teams. At some point, usually in the recovery room, I check a chest X-ray to make sure the lungs look good. This involves the radiologists again.

Teamwork is an efficient and productive way of approaching a common goal.

Even with such a big surgery, most patients recover quickly from the acute or critical aspects of the postoperative period and can often go to a regular patient floor where the nurses are comfortable taking care of patients who have had head and neck cancer surgery. Now a new nursing team enters the picture. Remember that the graft was taken from the patient's leg. We're eager to get the patient out of bed and moving, so physical therapists evaluate the patient and work with him to help him walk. Once the airway swelling has gone down, we remove the tracheostomy tube. When the graft has healed well enough, speech and swallowing therapists are involved to help the patient eat and drink, and help with speech issues that develop from such a surgery.

These patients may have trouble maintaining adequate nutrition because of the changes in their ability to eat. So before surgery, general surgery colleagues may place a temporary feeding tube into the stomach (a gastrostomy tube or G-tube). This allows us to start nutrition soon after the surgery.

Finally, the patient is able to go home. Our social service team helps set up discharge planning. The patient needs visiting nurses and physical therapy. He's still getting most of his nutrition via the G-tube, so we need to make sure he knows how to use the tube and that his insurance company is going to pay for the supplies for the tube as well as the tube feedings themselves. The patient needs help with dressing changes.

About three weeks after the surgery, the patient is ready to start daily radiation therapy. This lasts about seven weeks. He needs to coordinate rides to the radiation oncology department either with his family or through a service the hospital arranges. Once he has completed radiation therapy, he likely has some trouble swallowing from post-surgical and post-radiation changes in his neck that require more therapy. Also, he undergoes surveillance exams with me and the multidisciplinary head and neck clinic, periodic PET scans, and visits with plastics until everything is fully healed. The patient may develop an underactive thyroid from the radiation and metabolic changes related to changes in nutritional status, so his primary care provider remains an essential part of his care.

This is *one* patient! I omitted his inpatient and outpatient pharmacists. If he received chemotherapy, he would have had medical oncology nurses, oncology pharmacists, and the medical oncology doctors.

Two critical parts of the team are the patient and the patient's family/support network. The patient has to be willing to undergo the treatment and is an active participant in his care. The preparation before and the days of recovery, including physical therapy, swallowing therapy, speech therapy, and wound care, all require his full participation. The family helps provide the treatment, and assists with tube feedings, exercises at home, transportation to and from appointments and, most important, moral support.

You can see the level of teamwork that is essential in such a case. Within that teamwork are multiple "sub-teams"—the ablative surgery team, anesthesia team, plastics team, nursing team, and so on. Teamwork also happens in offices large and small, and typically there are other sub-teams, e.g., finances, marketing, and growth. Teamwork is essential in the military, the police department, the school system, your volunteer organization, even your household. These teams and their subsets arise because teamwork is an efficient and productive way of approaching a common goal.

Requirements of a Team

A team needs to have a common goal. Suppose I got together three phenomenal musicians, all virtuosos, and asked them to play together. Would the result be a great piece of music? Say each musician excels in a different genre—one jazz, one classical, and one rock and roll—and I ask each to play her favorite song, the song for which she's best known, all at the same time. All three songs are different, with different keys, time signatures, and tempos. The result will be cacophony. So even though I have the best musicians, each one has a separate goal—to play the piece of music each knows the best and performs the best—and the result is disastrous because the goal is not a common one. If instead I ask them to decide on a single song that they all know and can all perform together, their individual talents will be directed toward a common goal, performing that one song to the best of their individual abilities, and I suspect the result will be wonderful (albeit perhaps a bit unique).

In addition to a common goal, ideally the team should be composed of the right people. Suppose I present the common goal of winning a sports championship. I pick 11 athletes, all professional, world-class, hall-of-fame-quality basketball players. All are committed to winning a championship and have the competitive hunger that coaches love. The only problem is, the championship I'm asking them to win is the soccer World Cup Championship. There's a common goal, but I have the wrong people. One of my favorite books from the corporate world, Good to Great, by Jim Collins (2001, Harper Business), addresses this and speaks about having "the right people on the bus" to bring a company from good to great. This advice can be applied to any team situation.

For teamwork, we need a common goal and the right people to achieve that common goal. These are obvious, but from experience I've identified four additional elements that are essential to *successful teamwork—trust, communication, commitment,* and *attitude.* Whether you're about to remove a huge tumor from someone's neck or organize a band performance, trust, communication, commitment, and attitude are essential to the team's reaching its goals.

Trust

We'll discuss *Trust* here and address the other elements later in the book. One of the key reasons that my associates and I form a very successful team is that we trust each other. We trust each other to be ethical, caring, and skilled–in short, to be able to *do the right thing.* I have so much trust in the abilities and ethics of my associates that if we were working on a thyroid surgery on one of my patients, and in the middle of the case I were to pass out or collapse or drop dead, I'm certain my associate, an outstanding surgeon, would care for the patient and complete the surgery.

When I send a patient to someone more capable of a procedure, I trust that surgeon and respect his abilities and judgment. Putting ego and pride aside and recognizing someone is better at something than I am, are important parts of teamwork. My team's goal is to make sure the patient gets the best possible care, not to make sure that *I* do the surgery, or that *my* ego is stroked, or that *I* make more income. Trust and respect outweigh pride, ego, and personal gain.

> *Putting ego and pride aside and recognizing someone is better at something than I am, are important parts of teamwork.*

This may seem obvious, but it's critical. As doctors, we make sure our patients are able to get 24/7 care. Someone must always be on call, available to answer questions, or see a patient emergently. The person on call functions on behalf of all the physicians for whom she covers, whether or not they're her patients. This call arrangement is based on trust. Because I trust my associates and I respect their abilities, I know that when I'm not on call, my patients will receive excellent care.

Inherent in trust is *respect*. When we trust someone, we do so because we respect her skills, her decision-making, her ethics, and her level of compassion. Respect for a colleague's ability to perform as a valued and productive member of the team is essential to the team's success.

Another component of trust is the knowledge that my teammates have skill sets, ethics, and moral fabric worthy of respect. With trust in your team members, you can accept their recommendations, knowing they're based on the best interests of the team and its common goal. There's no concern about ulterior motives.

When we assemble the team, we can choose the right people, or as Jim Collins said, we can make sure we have the right people on the bus. But when individual personalities conflict, we may have to let someone off at the next bus stop.

Personality Types

There are may ways to categorize team personalities: passive aggressive, stubborn, "active" aggressive, and so on. The Myers Briggs Type Indicator (MBTI) comes to mind. In my experience on all kinds of teams, I've observed five personality types that describe most people and how they act most of the time. This is based strictly on my own experience, and takes into account my earlier discussion about fairness. My intent in describing these personality types is to suggest the balance of individual versus team goals within each type. I hope my ideas are useful additions in assessing team dynamics.

Understanding this distribution has helped me understand why conflicts occur, why I've succeeded in dealing with teammates, and why at other times I've failed miserably. Here are the five types.

> *My intent in describing these personality types is to suggest the balance of individual versus team goals within each type.*

Type 1. These are egocentric, self-centered, and focused on personal gain. They may be aggressive and insecure. They may undercut their colleagues and take credit for, or even steal their ideas. Their big picture is a zero-sum game. They are happiest when they win and others lose.

Type 5. These are the polar opposite, selfless and altruistic, always willing to "take one for the team." They may do the most work and be happy working from a broom closet to keep expenses down, but they never harbor resentment or expect reciprocity. You and I may want to think we're Type 5s. But I have to confess, if I'm always sacrificing and getting nothing in return, I'll feel resentful. It's human nature.

In Italian families, there's always someone who always does things for others. They act like they want nothing in return. They'll say: "I made you tomato sauce today, spent all day over the hot stove, making it just the way you like it. I don't mind doing it for you. I'd do anything for you. I'm just going to clean up now while you eat. Don't worry, I'll eat later if anything's left, or I'll just have a piece of bread and butter. It's no problem." Let me translate. "I slaved all day for you. See how hard I worked for you and how much I sacrificed? Think of this the next time you want to argue with me or forget to call when you're out late, or you want to go out with your friends instead of staying home and doing work around the house." We call this the "martyr."

I don't mean to disparage my Italian upbringing. I'm proud of it. But this sarcastic use of "martyr" is spot on. Type 5s are rare. Mother Teresa would be a Type 5. Self-centered Type 1s are also rare on teams. Maybe they don't manifest as true Type 1s, because they want to stay on the team.

These two types are at opposite ends of a Bell Curve. Types 2, 3, and 4 lie at the center, and describe most personalities on a team.

Type 2. They want the team to be successful and work toward the common goal, but always with a direct benefit in mind. Rarely do they suggest ideas that require sacrifice on their part. They're productive, but they always benefit, sometimes more than the team itself.

They are often the people with ideas who drive the team and push the envelope, because concern for their benefit also benefits the team. Others may look to them for knowledge and contributions, but may also resent them.

Type 3. This type falls right in the center. These members seek solutions that benefit the team and its members equally. An analysis of their ideas and actions over time shows a fairly even distribution of individual benefit and sacrifice. They are viewed as excellent team players.

Type 4. They put the team and its well-being first. They are excellent team players whose ideas and actions are driven by a desire to see the team succeed, and usually involve some compromise. They may even have a pattern of self-sacrifice. They're distinct from Types 2 and 3 in that they're always willing to give up something on behalf of the team.

However, unlike Type 5s, Type 4s expect *some* individual benefit for being team members, even if it's less than what others receive. Colleagues may caution Type 4s about being taken advantage of. In fact, if the issues of fairness discussed earlier are not addressed, Type 4s may become resentful, which would be counter-productive to the team.

Let's look at some of the potential interactions among these types. I won't talk much about Type 5s as I think they're rare, and gravitate to selfless positions like missionary and world hunger volunteer.

Consider a team with Types 2, 3, and 4. All agree on a common goal and have the skillset to achieve the goal. The Type 2 will be the driving force, the go-getter. The Type 3 may swing between self interest and compromise, but is generally on an even keel. Type 4 takes one for the team but still achieves some personal benefit. A team like this can work smoothly.

But the team should be aware that Type 4s who sacrifice to the point of feeling exploited can reach a boiling point. Addressing this, or ensuring a balance of compromise within the team, can help avert explosions. If you're a Type 4, be alert to feelings of resentment. I've been guilty of these.

It's beneficial for members to monitor their feelings about Type 2s, who seem to benefit from their actions on the team. Look for good ideas that don't directly benefit the Type 2s (who could benefit from more compromise and self-awareness.)

The Type 3 helps mediate and needs to be comfortable addressing others on the effect of their actions on the team and its members. Over time the Type 3 will benefit, compromise, and break even in equal proportions.

Type 1s are few and far between, and their presence on teams can create conflict. The idea of "team" is lost on them. We cannot expect them to change unless they're motivated to do so. Instead, we have to decide how we want to deal with them.

Take an extreme example. A rock star has an entourage: handlers, agents, make-up artists, stylists, and so on. But some are just hanging on, enjoying being around him, partying, and going to his shows. Let's assume our rock star enjoys their company. They worship the ground he walks on! But he doesn't care about them as team members. He's concerned only for his success. Does the hanger-on benefit? Sure, from the material benefits and from the social caché that goes with being friends with a rock star. Are there risks? Sure, because the rock star has no vested interest in the hangers-on. He could leave them behind in a moment's notice. This Type 1 has supporters, but the relationship is tenuous and maybe even parasitic—it's superficial and unhealthy.

How do the rest of us handle Type 1s? In their greed Type 1s can become paranoid, protect their turf, and hinder others' advancement. They may be insecure. They're toxic on teams just like perpetual complainers. Their toxicity is in part that we don't know how to deal with them. They seem to get what they want when they want it and receive better treatment. We seem to compromise for them, either because of their position, or because we don't want to deal with their behavior when they don't get their way.

So what can we do? We can ask why they bother us. Is it that they're a detriment to the team, or is the issue only with us? If we're concerned about fairness, we can redefine fairness as discussed earlier, or simply keep our distance. If we've tried this and the situation is still unworkable, we can try pointing out how their "Type 1 team personality" (as described by Lauretano) makes them difficult to work with. Or we can speak to a manager, or move on.

> *If you dislike me, I'd rather you tell me to my face than see you act as if you like me, only to discover you're telling others what a bad person I am.*

We should avoid talking about these people behind their backs. Don't try to rally a team against them. I've been guilty of this at one time or another and I've always regretted it. It's counterproductive and shows poor judgment and character. I always tell others, if you have a problem with me, tell me to my face. If you dislike me, I'd rather you tell me to my face than see you act as if you like me, only to discover you're telling others what a bad person I am.

Confrontation is more difficult than it seems. More often than not, nothing will change unless one key piece is in place: the Type 1 is willing to change. Think about this for a minute before you go on to the next paragraph. Think about people and their behaviors. Think about yourself and your own behaviors.

Too often we think we can change others. This applies everywhere—at home, in school, on the soccer team, in the orchestra. You can point out peoples' faults but you may not get the response you want. Don't be surprised if they retaliate or get defensive. They've worked within the framework of their

> *In using tools that can help us understand others and ourselves as we work toward common goals, we're doing the right thing.*

personality type for a long time and it's worked. They may rally other people against *you*. The rock star and CEO have supportive entourages who benefit. Type 1s may make small changes to placate others, but unless they're willing to make big changes, they'll revert to their old behaviors.

People can change, but they have to initiate the change and stick with it. Some patients with head and neck cancer from smoking have had their voice boxes removed and continue to smoke, either through their mouth (even though they can no longer inhale through their mouth), or through the trachea itself where it comes out of the neck. Their families, friends, and doctors encourage them to stop. We can urge change and offer support, but nothing will happen until they're ready to change.

Think about the "Serenity Prayer" (originally untitled) by theologian Reinhold Niebuhr, that Alcoholics Anonymous and other 12-Step programs have adopted.

God, grant me the serenity to accept the things I cannot change.
Courage to change the things I can.
And wisdom to know the difference.

This prayer is wise on the idea of change. What strikes me is the use of the word "I." Not "we," not "people," or "they," but "I." It's hard to change unless I am willing to change.

If a co-worker's behavior is problematic but not damaging and doesn't adversely affect the team, let it go. If the behavior is damaging, confront the person or speak to an appropriate arbitrator, but realize that there is no guarantee of results.

Constructive confrontation can help clear the air. But if there's no remedy, consider moving on.

Why didn't I mention the team member who is lazy, a "control freak," or passive-aggressive? Because any one of these individual personality types can be any of the five Team Personality Types. You can be a Type 4 and still be a control freak—you do most of the work because you think you have the best ideas and the best strategies. You can be lazy but still be a Type 1—you want all the benefits while everyone else does all the work. Maybe you're a Type 3—right in the middle, wanting the team to do well while you individually do well. But on the team, you're passive-aggressive in expressing your ideas or carrying out your tasks. You may go along in a negative way to show that you have a better way.

My interest is not so much in each individual personality type, but rather in using these Team Personality Types to understand how our interpersonal relationships and interactions with other team members can help the team succeed or fail. We can even use these Team Personality Types to predict whether our interpersonal relationships and interactions will contribute to failure or success in reaching a common goal. In using tools that can help us understand others and ourselves as we work toward common goals, we're doing the right thing.

ARTHUR LAURETANO

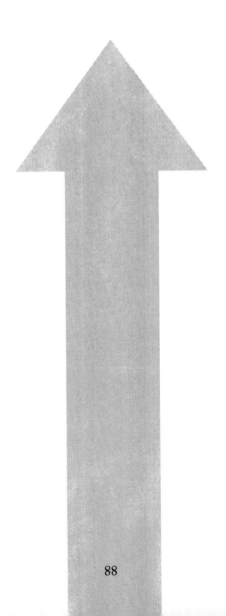

This chapter is about the impact we have on others, those close to us, and perhaps even those we've never met. It stresses how much we are interwoven into the fabric of society. Recognizing the impact we have on others is so important that I'm giving you homework assignments to convince you of the tremendous impact you have on others.

One of the most frequent procedures I do is *bilateral myringotomy and tubes*, or BMT—the placement of ear tubes for chronic ear problems. I usually do them on children who may be only a few months old, under general anesthesia. The procedure involves looking down the ear canal through a small, metal, funnel-like tube called an ear speculum. We use an operating room microscope that has an eyepiece similar to binoculars and gives a magnified view of the eardrum. I make a small incision in the eardrum, then insert a tube that equalizes pressure on both sides of the eardrum, preventing the buildup of fluid that contributes to decreased hearing and/or recurrent infections. It takes about 15 minutes. In the OR with me are one or two members of the anesthesia team, a circulating nurse, and a scrub nurse or scrub technician.

This procedure is one of the first we learn in residency and so straightforward a first-year resident can do it. So it's not uncommon for someone to say, "You have an easy day in the OR tomorrow, just a bunch of tubes." But I don't see it that way because of the impact of the procedure on the child and his family (it's often the child's first surgery), the impact of the circumstances that led to the procedure, and the impact of successfully performing the procedure. I also consider the impact if the procedure does not go well.

Let's consider the child who needs tubes. Alex is a 16-month-old boy who has had seven debilitating ear infections in the last five months. The last resulted in a febrile seizure, which frightened the family. Diarrhea or a yeast infection from the antibiotics gave him a severe diaper rash. When he gets an ear infection, he and his parents are up all night for one or two nights. The most recent infection required two injections of intramuscular Rocephin, an antibiotic injected into the thigh. Though the injection is often mixed with a local anesthetic to decrease the pain, it still hurts. Alex has become less responsive to voices, TV, and other sounds, indicating a decrease in hearing. Over the last *three* months, even between infections, his progress in developing words has tapered, and the few words he uses are less intelligible.

The pediatrician refers Alex and his family to me. At our first meeting, the parents are frightened, exhausted, and concerned about the recent seizure, the hearing loss, and the failure of some of the antibiotics.

Our smallest or simplest actions can have a profound effect on those around us.

Alex is a candidate for ear tubes, and I explain the benefits and risks of the procedure. The risk of the inhaled anesthesia is very low. There is a 1% chance of a hole remaining in the eardrum once the tube falls out (usually out about a year after placement), a very small risk of scarring of the eardrum, and a chance that Alex may need tubes again once the tubes fall out if his natural Eustachian tubes don't begin to function properly on their own.

The family decides to proceed. Consider the impact on their lives as we approach the surgery. One or both parents are anxious about Alex undergoing anesthesia and a surgical procedure. One or both arrange to take the day off from work for the surgery so they can be with Alex. Alex can't have anything to eat or drink for about four hours before the surgery, so the parents have to keep him occupied while he reminds them how hungry and thirsty he is.

One parent joins us in the OR. Alex breathes oxygen through a mask, anesthesia gas is added, and he falls asleep. It is tough for the parent to see this, but the child is quite comfortable. As a staff member escorts the parent to the waiting room, we hear her consoling words, "Don't worry. We'll take care of your child as if he were our own."

After about an hour in the recovery room, Alex and his family go home. Two weeks after the procedure, the parents report Alex is free from infections and sleeps through the night. He is hearing better. His vocabulary has increased and his balance has markedly improved. Some families have said, "It's like we have a new child."

This is one of the most enjoyable and gratifying procedures I do because of the tremendous positive effect it has on the child and his parents. I have had a major impact doing what most ENT surgeons would consider to be our *simplest operating room procedure.* The point of this chapter is that sometimes our smallest or simplest actions can have a profound effect on those around us.

You may think, "Arthur, you're crazy. You're a doctor; you're *expected* to have a dramatic impact on people." In *your* daily life, *your smallest action* can be just as significant.

Not convinced? Take this example. I took my son skiing for the first time. During a run down the bunny slope, I saw two ski instructors kneeling next to a young woman who was lying on the ground. When I saw the white crosses on their red jackets I realized they were the ski patrol/first aid team and the woman was lying on her side, in pain. When I got back to the top of the slope, I told my son to keep skiing while I checked on the woman. I identified myself as a physician to the two first aid personnel, and asked if I could be of assistance. I also explained I was an ENT surgeon and not a very good skier. (The woman said, "You're obviously a better skier than me!") They said I *could* be of assistance.

They were about to splint her arm, and asked me stay upslope to make sure no one skied into them. They lifted the woman onto a sled, handed me her skis and poles, and asked me to bring them down to the first aid station. I did that too. At the first aid station, I helped them transfer her to the stretcher. An ambulance took her to the hospital.

I got involved because, as a physician, I felt a responsibility to assist if I could. Nothing I did required being a surgeon. Except for knowing how to lift her from the sled to a stretcher without hurting her (and my back), the three things I did could have been done by anyone. I directed traffic, carried equipment, and helped carry someone from one stretcher to another. I had a positive impact. The young woman was grateful, her family was grateful, and the first aid personnel were grateful. I was probably one of the worst skiers on the slope that day, yet I was able to have a positive impact.

We are all capable of doing small, simple things that can have a significant impact. Consider the impact *you* have on others on a daily basis.

Do you coach a team of kids? You're teaching them the fundamentals of the sport, as well as teamwork and sportsmanship. You're teaching them the value of practice and the sense of pride and accomplishment from working hard and doing their best. You're teaching them how to learn from success and failure. Do you volunteer at your child's school? You're having a positive impact on *your* child, and the other children, the teachers, and the staff. People depend on you. Do you recycle? You are having a positive impact on the environment.

Much of what we do can have an effect on the world around us. The phrase, "Think global, act local" is attributed to Patrick Geddes in *Cities in Evolution* (1915, London: Williams). Its point is that even small, local changes or actions can contribute to global change.

Responsibility

What aspects of our actions have an impact on others? *Responsibility* is important. When I decide a child needs ear tubes, I'm accepting responsibility for taking care of that child. We mean it when we say, "We will take care of your child as if she were our own." When I'm operating on someone, that person becomes the most important person in the world to me.

When we take on a responsibility, we're making a *commitment* to complete the activity. We're accepting the consequences of our actions, whether positive or negative. If they're negative, we'll do our best to remedy them.

This may seem obvious for a surgeon. Here's how it applies more broadly. You offer to drive your 10-year-old son James and his friend Johnny home from school because Johnny's mother is working later than usual. You've made a commitment to be responsible for both boys. If Johnny comes to your house so the boys can go skateboarding, you make sure both wear the appropriate equipment. Johnny's mother is depending on you for her son's safety while he's with you, just as my patients depend on me.

Consider the idea of consequences. If I have a bad outcome with the surgery—say the wound opens up and does not heal well—I have to see it through, do everything I can to get that incision to heal. If I need help, the onus is on me to get that help.

Accountability

This leads me to *accountability*. When something goes wrong, some people try to try to cover things up, blame others, or say it wasn't their fault.

Most patients are a little nervous before surgery. No matter how well I explain it, it's still a mystery. People feel a loss of control. Some are concerned about *the accountability process*. They're concerned that if something goes wrong, the medical profession may somehow try to cover it up.

Patients ask questions about what we do when they're asleep. What do we talk about? Do we expose just the operating area? How will they know if something went wrong? When we operate, we follow multiple checklists. Anesthesia monitors the patient and records the values. Blood loss is monitored and recorded. All sponge, instrument, and needle counts must be correct at the end of the case to make sure that nothing is left in the patient. (For a great discussion of this process, see Dr. Atul Gawande's excellent work, *The Checklist Manifesto: How to Get Things Right*, Metropolitan Books, 2009.)

Any problems are reported to a peer-review board and undergo a peer-review process. In the hospitals where I work, cases are reported if the patients die or have serious adverse outcomes (heart attack, stroke, respiratory arrest). But cases may also be reviewed when there is unusual blood loss or the patient develops an infection.

In peer-reviewed cases, a group of physicians, nurses, and other staff goes over each case in detail to ensure everything met the standard of care. Even if the outcome is fine, there is dialogue with the involved physician(s), and corrective action is taken. At academic institutions where I've worked, this process is usually handled at M and M (Morbidity and Mortality) Rounds. (Some institutions call these D and Cs, or Deaths and Complications, also euphemistically know as Donuts and Coffee Rounds because of the free donuts and coffee served at the meeting.) Typically at M and Ms, a resident presents the case, then the residents and attendings are questioned about all aspects of the case. These are very honest, no-holds-barred discussions, and are both educational and humbling. This level of accountability is necessary: people's lives are at stake. Cases with even the slightest question can be brought to the peer-review process by other physicians, nurses and nursing support staff, scrub technicians, representatives from continuity of care, and even hospital administrators (perhaps because of a patient or family complaint). All cases are treated with the same diligence and scrutiny.

We should expect that we *will* be accountable for our actions, not that we may be accountable. Here's an example in which the action of one person impacts many people.

> *We should expect that we will be accountable for our actions, not that we may be accountable.*

Suppose you're the quality assurance inspector for a company that makes parts for airplane engines. The parts you inspect are so critical to the function of the engine that if you were to miss a defect in one part, and if that part ended up in an engine, that engine could fail midflight, leading to an airplane crash and the death of hundreds of people.

Think about the impact of this job. You commit to fully inspect each part. You understand the consequences if you miss a defective part. You understand that you could be held accountable if a defective part gets through. You inspect that engine part as if it were going into a plane that is carrying your children.

In the operating room, the surgeon is the "Captain of the Ship," the person responsible for all actions that affect the patient. When the patient has a good outcome, it's because every team member did his job; every person understood he was accountable for the patient's well-being. If something goes wrong, however, as the Captain of the Ship, I'm ultimately accountable.

It's easy to fall into the blame game. But it's counterproductive. It doesn't leave room to figure out how to prevent the problem. It undermines the teamwork and trust that are so important in our interactions with others. I'm impressed by coaches who praise their players when the team wins, and who accept the blame when their team loses.

Negative Impacts

Many "rules of medicine" are handed down as dogma because our predecessors learned, through experience, that diverging from these teachings can have bad outcomes. If you suspect that someone's airway is becoming compromised, and you're considering a tracheotomy, you more than likely should do the tracheotomy. A surgeon who hasn't been taught this rule may try to talk himself out of the procedure—he may not want to put the patient through it, or has another case he doesn't want to delay. In such cases, we follow the time-tested rule, because, as surgeons, we think through the worst- case scenario. We choose to make a pre-emptive strike.

So how does this apply to everyday activities? Consider this: Do you text when you drive? Or do you look over at your MP3 player to flip through your songs? Did a passenger in the car ever say she thought this was dangerous? Was your response something like: "I do this all the time and I've never had an accident" or "I just looked down for a second"? Public service messages tell us that the average time our eyes are off the road when texting is five seconds. Count out five seconds (one Mississippi, two Mississippi... you know the drill). At 65 miles an hour, you'd travel about 160 yards in five seconds; at 20 miles an hour (the speed you might travel in a neighborhood with kids) it's about 50 yards.

Suppose a young child runs out in front of your car during the five seconds your eyes are off the road and you kill that child. I could apply the same scenario to drinking and driving, or speeding.

This is so important I'm giving you three homework assignments.

HOMEWORK ASSIGNMENT 1:

Watch the local television news tonight. The top stories usually focus on bad news locally. Weather overview follows, then national and international news, and perhaps some politics. Then a detailed weather story, and perhaps some human interest or health story, then sports, and a feel-good story at the end. Pay particular attention to the beginning local news and final human-interest and feel-good stories.

Suppose the opening story is the murder of an innocent teenager caught in the crossfire of gang violence. Think about the impact of that event. This impact includes those close to the victim and the perpetrator, but also those affected by this story of *life being wasted*. These events hurt everyone in our society.

Now consider the positive human-interest story. Maybe a pastor in a community affected by gang violence has started a program to get kids into activities and off the streets. Maybe you donate. You and the pastor are having a positive impact.

Consider the idea of *six degrees of separation*, a concept articulated by the Hungarian writer Frigyes Karinthy, and showcased in John Guare's play of the same name. Everyone is, on average, six degrees away from everyone else in the world. *Nexus*, by Mark Buchanan (2002, Norton Publishing, New York) presents a similar theory. I met a woman from Japan at a Rock and Roll Fantasy Camp in New York in early 2011, and we exchanged email addresses. In 2011 a devastating earthquake and tsunami hit Japan near my friend's region. I emailed her and waited for a response. About a week later I learned she was alive and uninjured. The devastation was far from my little corner of the world, but the event still had a direct impact on me because it affected my friend. While I waited for news from her, my wife and I donated to the Red Cross efforts in Japan, hoping to make a positive impact. When you see such stories on the news, you feel for those involved and may offer some form of help.

HOMEWORK ASSIGNMENT 2:

Next time you are at the mall or at a sporting event or concert, look at those around you. All make an impact in their daily lives. One may be a special education teacher or a police officer. Look at the father and mother taking their children to their first baseball game. Did they have to work extra hours to pay for the tickets? And the game—what a great experience for the children!

Thinking of our interconnectedness brings to mind Hillary Clinton's book, *It Takes a Village* (Simon and Shuster, 1996). The title comes from an old African proverb, "It takes a village to raise a child." Think about the saying, "If you give a man a fish, you feed him for a day. If you teach a man to fish, you feed him for a lifetime." Teach someone to be self-sufficient, and she can thrive and excel on her own. As members of a community, we have opportunities to help each other and to receive help.

If we're receiving help, we have an obligation to try to get back on our feet. I think the village has the right to expect that once I'm better, I'll be back to work, providing for myself and my family, and helping someone else in the village who is in need.

> *With every bottle you recycle, every door you hold for someone, and every time you thank someone, you're making a positive, cumulative contribution.*

On a more positive note, I'm impressed by people who appreciate the help they've received, and give back to their community of origin. I know of physicians who grew up in impoverished areas and because they were given a chance, went back to practice in those communities.

Even the smallest good deed has positive impact. With every bottle you recycle, every door you hold for someone, and every time you thank someone, you're making a positive, cumulative contribution.

HOMEWORK ASSIGNMENT 3:

Part A. Think of the positive impacts you've had on others. Then consider the possible far-reaching effects of these actions.

Here's a little motivation. In Frank Capra's classic American movie *It's a Wonderful Life*, George Bailey (played by Jimmy Stewart) falls upon hard times as his company runs into financial issues. He contemplates suicide on Christmas Eve but is thwarted by his guardian angel, Clarence Odbody, who hears George say he wishes he'd never been born.

Clarence shows George what life would have been like without him. The town of Bedford Falls would have become Pottersville, owned and controlled by Mr. Henry F. Potter, a slumlord. The local pharmacist would have ended up in jail for accidentally poisoning a child. Then Clarence and George look at the tombstone of George's younger Harry, who as a child fell through the ice. Clarence tells him, "Your brother, Harry Bailey, broke through the ice and was drowned at the age of nine." George retorts, "That's a lie. Harry Bailey went to war! He got the Congressional Medal of Honor! He saved the lives of every man on that transport." Clarence delivers the knockout punch. "Every man on that transport died! Harry wasn't there to save them, because you weren't there to save Harry." George understands the scope of his impact and wants to live.

Now, have your "George Bailey moment." Think about all the times you've had a positive impact–the times you have helped out, made a difference in someone's life. Don't underestimate yourself. Don't underestimate the long-term and far-reaching impact one small act can have.

Part B. Think of negative impacts you may have had. Maybe the act was something as harmless as a negative comment. When I was five years old, the lady down the street told my mother I'd never amount to anything. My mother was very upset. Many times I could have held my tongue. Remember that seemingly small negative acts can have far-reaching consequences.

Part C. Look at times when your inaction may have led to a negative outcome. This may be the hardest part to discuss. My examples scare me.

In medicine, there are always cases that involved debates about doing a procedure versus watching and waiting. There have been times when, in hindsight, it would have been prudent to proceed with surgery.

One Friday night after finishing my cases, I stopped on my way home to get coffee in the hospital lobby. Rounds had included seeing a patient in the ICU (we'll call him Mr. Smith). He seemed to be doing fine. I wasn't on call, so my day should've been over. I was just about to leave, go home to have dinner, and then go to band practice, but I heard a STAT page calling the ICU doctor and the respiratory team to the ICU. I paused a few feet from the revolving door that stood between me and my weekend. Then I thought, "What if that page is for Mr. Smith? Maybe his airway is obstructing or maybe he's bleeding." Then I had another thought, "Hey, you're not on call. Your day is done. The ICU doctors can take care of that. If he needs an airway, anesthesia can do it or they can call the doctor on call."

At this point I felt I was in a movie with an angel on one shoulder and a devil on the other. Another thought came to mind, "It's six o'clock; your partner who's on call is probably at home or at least sitting in traffic." So I ran to the ICU because I decided this was the right thing to do. Mr. Smith was sitting up in bed, watching TV, and waving to me with a big smile on his face. But two rooms down the hall, a crowd of nurses and doctors worked on a patient whose neck and face were swollen and whose airway was closing. Anesthesia could not get a breathing tube in, and the patient's oxygen levels were dangerously low. She was likely to go into cardiopulmonary arrest (no breathing and no pulse).

I performed an emergency cricothyrotomy to secure the patient's airway. One of the nurses said, "Thank God you were still in the hospital!" The patient did fine and was sent home a few days later. This case shows the possible consequences of inaction. Because I checked out the situation, I saved a life.

Let's consider everyday examples. You're walking down the street and see someone across the street leave a bag on a bench. You consider running across the street to retrieve the bag and return it but you're late for work. Suppose the bag contains the one holiday gift the person could afford. What if someone else finds the bag and it becomes "finders keepers"?

Suppose someone falls on the sidewalk. You're the only one nearby. Would you run over to help or call 911 and wait until help shows up? Or, worried about personal liability, would you do nothing? Such thoughts may lead us to inaction.

Multitasking

Let's think about the implications of multitasking. Why do we think it's okay to do anything else but drive while we're driving? We think it's *an accomplishment to multitask.* It's not infrequent to hear someone brag about how well he can multitask, or criticize a co-worker who can't.

I know people who drive and hold the steering wheel with a knee, with a coffee in one hand and a cell phone in the other, and somehow keep the wheel stable. People talk on the cell phone while paying the cashier at the supermarket, or type on the computer with one hand while thumbing through the newspaper, organizing a briefcase, or eating lunch.

Multitasking is not new. My mother cooked dinner, helped me with my homework, and at the same time carried on a phone conversation with my maternal grandmother. She was like some kind of "kitchen octopus." Today, computers allow us to open up multiple reports or flip through several presentations at once. Though multitasking isn't new, we seem to place more value on it today. This got me thinking, "When does multitasking work and when doesn't it?"

Multitasking works best when our activities are directed toward a common goal and when we're able to do each activity as well as if it were the only activity. Here's an operating room example. When I'm doing a thyroidectomy, I'm focused on the patient's neck, the thyroid gland in particular. I wear operating loupes that magnify the surgical field, so I have a sense of tunnel vision focused on the thyroid. We're usually talking during the surgery, not only about the case, but perhaps about our families, a recent football game, or plans for next weekend. But what I'm listening to more intently is the sound of the oxygen saturation monitor and the EKG monitor that are connected to my patient. Music may be playing in the operating room, but I'm in tune with the monitors. Also, as my hands are operating, I'm hitting the on-off switch for the cautery instrument with my foot. In other words, my hands, my ears, my eyes, even my feet are working together for one goal—to perform the best surgery I can. If we get to a difficult part of the case and the conversation or the music becomes a distraction, it stops. I need my brain, eyes, hands, ears, and feet to do surgery.

> *Multitasking works best when our activities are directed toward a common goal.*

Bottom line: there's nothing wrong with multitasking, but understand your limits, and within those limits, make sure the multitasking contributes to a common goal.

Consider what we've discussed regarding having an impact, of being responsible, recognizing your commitments, and accepting the consequences of your actions. Consider that you may have a positive impact on others, yet may not always be the one credited. President Harry S. Truman said: "It is amazing what can be accomplished if you do not care who gets the credit." Don't worry about getting credit; have the positive impact anyway.

Consider your motivation for helping others. Don't fall into the trap of helping people only if they owe you. I love the scene in *Rocky III* when Rocky (Sylvester Stallone) and Paulie (Burt Young) are leaving the police station and Paulie is arguing with Rocky. Rocky states, "Nobody owes nobody nothin'. You owe yourself." Paulie argues, "You're wrong! Friends owe!" Rocky retorts, "Friends don't owe! They do because they wanna do." You don't keep what I call a "favor ledger"—a kind of Ebenezer Scrooge accounting book of who owes whom a favor. To quote a line from Billy Swan's song I Can Help, "It would sure do me good, to do you good. Let me help."

Regarding negative impact: Remember *Primum non nocere*— "First, do no harm?" I've learned to apply this when I'm caring for a patient and in other life situations. I don't want a student to regret I was her teacher, or a player to regret I was his coach. I don't want to be viewed as having had a negative impact because of a negative action or failure to act.

We can think globally and act locally. We can affect the world around us, one small act at a time. We can fill the pitcher of water that is the greater good by contributing one small drop at a time. I believe that when we consider the impact on others and strive to make that impact positive, we'll do the right thing.

Chapter Nine:
COMMUNICATION AND TIME

Now we move on to communication, highly relevant to our discussion of teamwork. Transparency among members is of paramount importance to good communication; it fosters productive teamwork. What do I mean by transparency?

Transparency

Suppose I'm in a practice with two other people, and we have two corner offices and one that is the size of a broom closet. In two years, the practice is moving to a new office space with two corner offices and one gigantic office with a large window and a beautiful panoramic view. Say I decide to take one for the team and take the broom closet for the time being. In the back of my mind, I'm

> *Had I been transparent, I might not have gotten what I wanted, but I'd have no false expectations that later might have become a source of resentment.*

thinking that by volunteering now, when we move to the new office, my associates will feel that I deserve the largest office. But when we move my associates say we'll put our names in a hat and draw for the gigantic office. Remember our discussion of fairness?

I have no right to be angry or upset because, when I offered to take the broom closet I didn't stipulate that I expected in the new space to get the largest office. I wasn't transparent. Had I specified this my associates might have agreed, or said we'll draw names, as this is a new beginning for all of us. Had I been transparent, I might not have gotten what I wanted, but I'd have no false expectations that later might have become a source of resentment.

Let's move from the hypothetical to the realistic. My goal in starting the head and neck multidisciplinary clinic at our hospital was to provide multidisciplinary care to our cancer patients with better and more coordinated care and fewer visits. My goal was not to make more money. We set the clinic up on Thursdays, my day out of the office. As the clinic grew, it became a regular part of my schedule, every other Thursday morning. A medical practice financial consultant would have said I could make more money seeing patients during that time. But my goal was not a financial one.

The clinic has been very successful and extremely gratifying. The hospital administration made me its medical director and now pays me for that service. Why do I tell you this? Because I was transparent in my communications with the hospital. My goal was to set up a successful clinic. I never thought, "I'm going to do this clinic for free for three years, then go to the hospital administrators and say that I expect payment." While I might have sounded greedy, at least all the cards would have been on the table. The key is transparency in communication. It leaves no room for assumptions, hidden agendas, or ulterior motives.

Another example comes from the summer before junior year when I worked in patient transport at a local hospital. At night I went to the optional soccer practices and conditioning sessions held by the high-school soccer coach, as I'd planned to play soccer again in the fall. When the mandatory week of soccer camp approached, I explained to my boss at the hospital that I wouldn't be available for that week of work. She told me I had to work, and if I didn't, I'd lose the job. So I explained that to the soccer coach. I'd assumed that, as I'd gone to all of the optional practices, he'd still take me on the team. WRONG! I can still see his face when he told me, "How do you expect to make the team if you don't come to camp?"

I was devastated, then angry. Here I was, trying to secure my future in medicine and save money, and I was being punished by not being able to play soccer. How could my boss not realize that I was a hard-working 16-year-old who just needed one week off? My anger was directed at the coach and my boss, but the person at fault was me. I should've informed both people of my wishes much earlier on.

Teams may be a business, an athletic team, an orchestra, or a family. In all these teams, communication is essential. The team must decide how to communicate, and transparency must be part of its goal.

Voice Your Opinion

When a team discusses a direction, it should encourage all members to be transparent and express an opinion. Do your best to express your ideas rather than abstaining or sitting on the fence. This works better in the long run.

Why do I say this? I've heard team members say they're comfortable with whatever direction the team chooses. I've done this myself when I didn't have strong feelings. By default, I accepted the team's decision. And I forfeited the right to later criticize that decision. A line in the song "Free Will" by the band Rush: says, "If you choose not to decide, you still have made a choice." If you don't make a choice, you may be forfeiting the ability to have further impact on the decision.

You've seen people who don't express their ideas, then when things don't go their way, deliver the silent treatment. This makes the whole office uneasy. You've seen people who try to sabotage ideas they didn't agree with by being passive-aggressive, or actively aggressive. Mark Sanborn, who speaks and writes on leadership and teamwork, says, "In teamwork, silence isn't golden, it's deadly."

If you were in the minority in supporting an idea that later turned out to be the better one, avoid the temptation to say, "I told you so." Instead, realize that others will see you as a "go-to" person for more ideas and insight. If your idea is chosen and it works well, don't gloat. Simply be glad you've been able to benefit the team.

What if you present an idea everyone shoots down? Then later, someone else proposes the same thing and everyone's on board. It's natural to want to say "Wait a minute, that was my idea and no one liked it!" You might feel insulted. You might ask, "Did they think it was a bad idea because I said it? Is there something bad about the way I present things, or do people not trust or respect me?"

> *In teamwork, silence isn't golden, it's deadly.*

I've been in this position. I've learned that people often need time to process things before they can buy into an idea. People may need to hear the idea in their own words. The important thing is to realize that it doesn't matter whose idea it was, as long as it's good for the team. President Harry S Truman stated, "It is amazing what you can accomplish if you do not care who gets the credit." (Several sources listed the author of this as anonymous, but other sources stated it was Harry S. Truman.)

Choose Your Battles

Sometimes you'll want to make your case even in the face of strong opposition. Be alert to times when by compromising, you can achieve much of your goal. Your compromising will help create an environment where others are wiling to do the same. Some people love to play the "devil's advocate." This can be thought-provoking and make us alert to more ramifications of a decision. But being contrarian just for its own sake can be counterproductive. To some extent, it comes down to how you do it.

I've learned to pay attention to my emotions in heated discussions. If my emotions are starting to get the better of me and I'm feeing argumentative or hostile I try to use the "three-second delay" from radio talk shows. I try to self-censor before I open my mouth. If I let issues build up without expressing them in a constructive and productive manner, I tend to "explode." I find myself yelling, bringing up things that seem totally out of the blue. Before I turn a workable situation into a disaster, I assess what I'm about to say and where my emotions are going. If you don't think a battle is worth undertaking, it's better to compromise early. You'll appear more reasonable, more gracious, and more understanding. If a battle is worth fighting, do so with tact, professionalism, and diplomacy.

These principles also apply to couples. Again, transparency is key. Here are some approaches that lack transparency: the passive-aggressive approach (I'll do this the way he wants it even though I see a major flaw in his idea, just so I can show him how stupid he is), the mixed message (the husband who tells his wife she can go out with her friends one night, then when she comes home, he says to her, "I can't believe you went out tonight and didn't spend the night with me"), and the double-standard (for example, if I told my wife she couldn't spend money on new curtains because we are trying to save money, but then I go out and buy yet another guitar). I'm not a marriage or relationship expert, but if you've ever stepped back to analyze relationships, you can immediately see how complex such teams can be and how essential communication is.

Encourage Others

In team communication it's important to encourage others. It's easy to find fault and criticize; it can be harder to praise. Our own insecurities may be at play. We may fear someone will get a bigger reward. When I think this way, I recall the ideas in the chapter "Finances and Fairness." The team, its efforts, and the praise that individuals receive aren't a zero-sum game. When someone does a good job for the team, she benefits the entire team, and therefore benefits you as a team member. Thanking your teammates and co-workers goes a long way toward creating a successful team environment.

Commitment

Commitment to the team and to its goals is another essential element of strong and successful teamwork. When I'm removing a tumor from someone's neck, I expect that everyone on the team is committed to removing that tumor. When I help one of my associates do a large head and neck case, I'm committed to helping her reach the goal of removing that patient's cancer. That patient is now also my patient. I don't get concerned about who gets credit

> *Commitment drives us to set aside our differences and forget about egos.*
> *It encourages others to use their strengths and helps them overcome their weaknesses.*

for the surgery, or who gets paid more, or how many times I've helped someone.

Commitment drives us to set aside our differences and forget about egos. It encourages others to use their strengths and helps them overcome their weaknesses. It allows us to discover how we can best use our strengths to support the team.

Group Projects

As a Type A, obsessive-compulsive kid, I hated group projects in school. It always seemed that at least one person on the team didn't do his part. There were usually two options. One: let it go, and know the final project will be deficient. The whole team suffers. Two: the other members pick up the slack. The final grade will be satisfactory and the slacker gets equal credit. If you're like me, you'd choose the second option, because in option one the whole team suffers.

In medical school I was part of a group presentation about vocal cord disorders. One member didn't do his part. I ended up doing his part and mine. I felt taken advantage of, but remembered the team's goal. On the day of the presentation, the slacker presented the material I'd put together for him. He fumbled through it and didn't know what one of the slides illustrated. He asked me. I explained it was a picture of diseased vocal cords. Then he had trouble fielding questions. Later, a few of the professors told me it was obvious who'd done the work. And over time they gave me a lot of extra opportunities and responsibilities that allowed me to get an Honors for that clinical rotation.

When we do team surgeries in practice, typically the larger cancer surgeries, one of the doctors is the patient's main doctor who took histories, did exams and tests, discussed the diagnosis, and recommended surgery. The other doctors assist. This may suggest the senior surgeon performs the main and most complicated parts of the surgery. But in a lot of practices, particularly community practices such as ours, the primary surgeon and assistant surgeon are both very experienced surgeons. Both are equally committed to the patient. If I have a better angle to view the tumor and cut around it, I do it. If my associate is in a better position to make the cut, and I'm able to retract for him to do that, that's how we do it. We are both committed to the surgical team and its goal—to cure the patient's cancer by surgical therapy.

Delegating

If you're tempted to take on a team project, avoid the temptation to do it all yourself. Team projects involve a significant work load and require delegating tasks. An important part of being on a team, especially as a leader, is being able to delegate to others and letting them approach the task as they see fit. You can offer suggestions and help, but avoid the pitfall of expecting them to do things exactly as you would. This makes you a control freak.

I'm impressed by hospital administrators who let those in lower positions approach tasks in their own way. Successful administrators often use the term "directionally correct" when an outcome is not as expected: "Your plan to improve the hospital's bottom line last month fell short by $200,000, but the approach was directionally correct. Let's reevaluate the strategy you used and see where we can make some corrections." This is a far cry from saying to your employee: "You lost $200,000? How could you be so stupid? I knew I should have done this myself!"

The idea of commitment as important to teamwork is not new. Margaret Mead said, "Never doubt that a small group of thoughtful, committed people can change the world. Indeed, it is the only thing that ever has." And Babe Ruth put it this way, "The way a team plays as a whole determines its success. You may have the greatest bunch of individual stars in the world, but if they don't play together, the club won't be worth a dime."

Attitude

My final requirement for a strong team is attitude. Those who know me well would laugh at me for writing this section, because I've not always gone to work with the best attitude. When I'm an hour behind and the phone is ringing and I have to do an emergency procedure in the office, you might hear me muttering how much I hate my job.

A negative attitude is counterproductive and a drain on my teammates. A negative attitude can become contagious and infect the office like a virus. A negative member may look for allies. Positive members may distance themselves. An outsider may judge a negative member as representative of the whole team. The result: a divided, dysfunctional team.

I try to evaluate the issues that harm my attitude and find ways to fix them, like changing my schedule to avoid falling behind.

> *The way a team plays as a whole determines its success. You may have the greatest bunch of individual stars in the world, but if they don't play together, the club won't be worth a dime.*

I try to compartmentalize stressors and not take work home, or let home pressures impinge on work. Much of what we consider success or failure in an individual or team is based not on external factors, but on internal ones, like attitude.

ARTHUR LAURETANO

One-on-One Communication

When I walk in to see my patients, I greet them by name and introduce myself. I ask about their problems and their symptoms. As I listen, I type what they tell me into my laptop. Fortunately, I can type well enough to maintain eye contact. The most important part of any communication is listening.

The patient may speak for only a few minutes, but I gain a wealth of information. The patient becomes more comfortable speaking with me and builds rapport. I want the patient to feel—through my body language, eye contact, and demeanor—that I'm fully attentive, not in a rush, and not disinterested.

How much time do you think elapses before I start to ask questions? According to a study by Marvel, Epstein, Flowers, and Beckman in the *Journal of the American Medical Association* (JAMA) published January 1999 (JAMA 1999 Jan 20; 281 [3]:283-7), the average time until the physician redirected (they did not use the word interrupted) the patient's opening statement was 23.1 seconds. The study found that patients who completed their statements without redirection used only "six additional seconds more on average" than those who were redirected. The consequences of incomplete descriptions included "late-arising concerns and missed opportunities to gather potentially important patient data."

When I go to the doctor I get a little nervous about making sure I provide all pertinent details. If I'm interrupted, I may forget something, only to remember it as I leave. We call this the doorknob comment—"Oh, by the way, I forgot to tell you I had some chest pain the other day, but we can discuss that next time." Overlooking such a symptom could result in there not being a next time!

Our doctor's appointment is for a limited time and we feel pressured to make sure we cover everything. Maybe we're embarrassed about a problem and need to get through a few simpler things before we state what is really bothering us. Consider the following. I walk into my doctor's office and start explaining my symptoms. "Yes, Dr. Jones, over the last year I've gained a little weight and I want to make sure my thyroid is fine. I've had a few muscle aches but attribute those to karate. I've been a bit more tired since I started working the night shift. My wife thinks I should have my cholesterol checked because my dad's cholesterol was high at my age. I also wanted to ask . . ." (it took me about 23 seconds to say all that). Dr. Jones interrupts to ask if I've ever had thyroid problems and whether there's a family history. We discuss thyroid disease and treatments. He asks about my sleep habits. Do I snore? Has anyone noticed I stop breathing during sleep? He checks my thyroid, and plans to run blood tests.

The problem is that I had one more thing to say before he interrupted me. I wanted to add: "I need to talk about erectile dysfunction. Recently I have been having trouble initiating or maintaining an erection, and it's affecting my marriage." That was my final and most important concern, but I was embarrassed to bring it up right away.

Listening

Listening is the key to good communication. Interrupting sends a negative message. It tells the speaker, "You're not telling me the information fast enough. What you're saying isn't important. I have other things to do, so let's cut to the chase."

When we speak, we want four things to occur. They comprise what I consider to be the skill of *Listening* or "The Global Concept of Listening." Here are my key points.

- We want people to **hear** us.
- We want people to **listen** to us. We want people to be attentive, to register and process what we're saying.
- We want to be **understood**.
- Ideally, we want others to **agree** with us.

Hearing and listening are different skills. Frank Tyger, editorial cartoonist for The Trenton Times, stated: "Hearing is one of the body's five senses. But listening is an art."

In medicine we talk about empathy when we're discussing communication skills. Not sympathy, but *empathy*. *Webster's Dictionary* defines empathy as "the understanding of and intellectual identification with the attitudes, feelings, or thoughts of others." Sympathy, on the other hand, is defined as "kindness of feeling toward one who suffers; pity; commiseration; compassion." Even if others don't agree with us, if we've been heard, listened to, and understood, then we've successfully expressed ourselves.

> *Hearing is one of the body's five senses. But listening is an art.*

When I'm talking with a patient about surgery, I want her to hear me (no distractions or noise drowning me out), to be attentive, and to understand why I want to proceed with surgery, what the surgery will entail, and so on. If this is what I expect when I speak as a physician, why would I interrupt the patient 23.1 seconds into the encounter when *she* is speaking?

If you're a good *listener*, you'll be *speaking with* someone as opposed to *talking at* them. I can gauge if someone is talking at me by using what I call "Arthur Lauretano's Cardboard Cutout Rule." Here's how it works. Suppose I think someone is talking at me. If I replaced myself with a cardboard cutout and walked away, and the person continued talking to the cardboard cutout, I'd know I was being talked at. Remember the scenes in the movie "Airplane!" (1980), when Robert Hays' character, Ted Striker, tells the passengers sitting next to him about his past with his girlfriend Elaine (Julie Hagerty)? The stories are so boring that his seatmates commit suicide. But Striker keeps talking.

I try to self-assess my own conversations to make sure that I'm engaging in true *dia*logue. My goal is not to present a *mono*logue but to truly engage in a mutual interchange of speaking and listening.

Thinking about how we want others to listen to us can help us be better listeners. Jimi Hendrix said, "Knowledge speaks, but wisdom listens." The 1924 English Gold Medal Olympian Doug Larson put it this way, "Wisdom is the reward you get for a lifetime of listening when you'd have preferred to talk."

Body Language

What makes face-to-face communication special? Physical presence. I gain a lot from sitting with the patient, establishing a rapport, and watching her body language, just as she watches mine. I learn from the quality of her voice whether she has a laryngeal (voice box) disorder. The distress in her presentation is a clue to the severity of her symptoms.

I've learned to make sure that I look attentive. I sit back comfortably while my patients speak, even while I'm typing, to convey that I'm relaxed but attentive, that I'm listening, and I'm not going to interrupt within 23.1 seconds and start my exam.

When I feel the urge to jump in with a question before someone has finished, my body language gives it away—my muscles tense. I try to stop myself. I'm trying to apply this to my conversations outside the patient-doctor relationship, particularly with my wife, the one I interrupt the most.

Imagine I've just texted or emailed you the sentence "Have a nice day." I might mean it. I could put a smile after it. Maybe I'm having a bad day so I follow it with a frown. Maybe you and I are arguing and I intend it sarcastically. In face-to-face communication, my intent would be clear from my body language and tone of voice, inflection, volume, and pace.

Pitfalls of Social Media

We are social animals. We need to interact with each other. Social media provide new ways to do so. The principles of Listening also apply to email, text messaging, and social networking. We can be heard, because we have a huge audience. When someone responds to our posts, we know someone is listening. And unlike face-to-face conversation, we can't be interrupted. We can transmit our entire thought.

A downside to texting and emailing is the limited ability to express emotion and the difficulty of assessing it. Explosions happen. I've seen business deals end because of angry email. When we write an email message, particularly a hostile or argumentative one, why are we so quick to hit send? Why not read it over a few times?

The problem with email is that we can't take it back. (In spoken conversation we know when something is going wrong and can deal with it in minutes.) As well, email carries a sense of anonymity. We're not face-to-face with our correspondent. It's the same principle that makes people feel safer swearing at us when they're in their car, not standing right in front of us. Also, when we compose an angry email, our emotion feeds on itself and gains momentum. We go on and on, adding fuel to the fire. We can easily reread, edit, and reconsider electronic communications. Instead we fire them off.

The situation worsens exponentially. But we claim we never intended it to sound so bad. We wrote it when we were stressed, or angry at something else, or didn't understand some important fact, or were tired. We wrote it, then regretted it.

I call this "The Paradox of Electronic Communication." In spoken conversation we tend to use filters. Almost paradoxically, we seem to be more afraid to say something derogatory, inflammatory, or hostile than to write it. We may be too shy, too embarrassed, too intimidated, or too diplomatic. We'd rather put it in an email or text message even though we create an electronic paper trail and permanent record. Things you've written and sent can be tracked down in many ways.

> *The problem with email is that we can't take it back.*

Consider to whom you're sending your email message. I can't tell you how many times I've received a group email or text and looked at the list of recipients and said, "This email is saying a lot of negative stuff about Jane, and it's written as if Jane isn't a recipient, but Jane is the third name in the recipient list." Take home message: Beware the "Reply All" button. Look above the body of your email and check the recipients.

How many times have you read someone's posts on social media and said, "I can't believe he posted that. What if his boss sees it?" When you post something, always assume your boss will see it. Consider this when you decide what to post publicly and what to share confidentially.

Why don't we use the "save-as-draft" feature of email more often? It's a strength of email communication, something like the three-second delay. My challenge is to figure out a way to apply the "save-as-draft" concept to email and face-to-face conversations.

The "save-as-draft" principle applies more broadly. I was raised to never go to bed angry with someone. In an Italian Catholic family, guilt may play a large part in this. What if the person you're mad at dies in the middle of the night and you never get to apologize? Here's another perspective. We're in the middle of an argument and bedtime approaches. It's probably better to pick up the discussion the next day with cooler heads, rather than rush into a hasty solution.

> *We have two ears and one mouth so that we can listen twice as much as we speak.*

We learn a lot from going back over things, contemplating options, and rethinking our concerns. When we get the chance to reconsider things, in email, face-to-face conversation, or even actions, we should take advantage of them to make sure what we write, say, or do is truly what we mean.

Some of my patients go to blogs when they're considering surgery. I love informed patients, and am happy to answer questions. But I'm amazed that people seem to find more negative things on line than positive ones. People blog about the pain of the surgery or the scar, or say "Don't let your doctor use this technique."

But even before people surfed the web, this was the same. Patients would come in and say things like, "My sister told me not to have surgery for my cancer, because once air hits the cancer, the cancer spreads." That isn't true, yet many people believe it.

Why is this? We want to be helpful to those with cancer, but maybe we're afraid of surgery. What we're doing is projecting our own fears onto the cancer patient. Also, we're sometimes willing to express our displeasure with something (and certainly more quickly) than our satisfaction. Department stores used to have complaint departments, but not compliment departments. Now they're called customer service.

Blogs make it easy to quickly transmit negative comments. True, we can express positive ones, but I'm probably quicker to fill out a survey to expresses complaints than to express praise. I've become more diligent about giving positive feedback after learning that people rely on survey responses for promotions or bonuses, and I remember "save-as-draft" before firing off something angry. Again, we need to be sure that when we express ourselves, we think out all the consequences.

A quotation on the importance of listening stands out. It comes from Epictetus (teacher of Stoicism, AD 35-AD 135): "We have two ears and one mouth so that we can listen twice as much as we speak."

Time

A patient was extremely upset with me because I kept him waiting for an hour before I saw him. He let me know as soon as I walked into the room. He said I had no respect for his time, that "you doctors" schedule too many patients, and that "you doctors" think your time is more valuable than everyone else's. He vowed never to come back. He also vowed to tell his primary care doctor not to refer patients to me. I tried to explain why I was running behind. I found myself saying "That's medicine." It may have come across as "Hey, that's life, take it or leave it." The patient posted a negative review of me on a blog, declaring I was unapologetic, and that

I just kept saying, "That's medicine." Now, let me tell you the whole story.

It happened on a day that I'm usually in the operating room, but didn't have any cases scheduled. I was on call so came into the office to see emergency patients and those who wanted earlier appointments. Then I received an emergency call from another hospital. A passenger in a bus involved in an accident had struck his neck across the top of the hard seat in front of him and been brought in by ambulance. He was on aspirin, which thins the blood, and was starting to have trouble breathing. He appeared to be developing a hematoma (collection of blood) around the airway. They needed me immediately to secure the airway because the anesthesiologists didn't think they'd be able to get a breathing tube into the patient. I left the office, leaving my patients in the exam rooms and waiting room, and told my secretary to reschedule the morning patients to another day. I performed an emergency tracheotomy and we saved the patient's life. I got back to the office about 1 p.m. I planned to see my afternoon patients.

Unbeknownst to me, some of the morning patients had stuck around to be seen. A cancer patient thought he had recurrent cancer and needed to be seen. I couldn't turn him away. Another patient wanted to go over his hearing test. I thought this would be brief. But he was also concerned about a lymph node that might be cancerous, and needed to discuss stress-related issues. I couldn't turn him away because these issues were important and I wanted to treat the whole patient. I finally got to see my 1 p.m. patient at 2 p.m. This was the patient who wrote the negative blog entry about me.

I introduced myself and said, "How are you doing?" The answer was, "Not well. You've no respect for my time or the time of others.

I've been waiting for an hour to see you. Obviously you scheduled too many patients." I apologized and calmly explained that I had to leave emergently to do a tracheotomy on a patient whose airway was closing off. I have to admit that I expected the patient to say he understood. Instead he continued to "lay into me." I was getting defensive, and tried to explain that sometimes in my field, we get called away for emergencies. As I got flustered, I began to condense my thoughts about the inherent unpredictability of medicine into the phrase, "that's medicine."

I do fall behind in the office, and I hate it. It's not that I don't have respect for other people's time. What I am guilty of is respecting the time of the person I'm with. I listen to the whole story—I believe in the holistic approach. A cancer patient confided that he was in an abusive relationship and afraid he might not get to his radiation treatments. We set up social services and helped get him into safety. Taking in the whole picture takes time.

I ran behind one day because a surgeon who had done a tongue biopsy referred his patient. I looked at the reports and said, "Dr. X was kind enough to refer you to me for treatment of the tongue cancer he diagnosed. I've read the reports and this is very treatable. I am very optimistic that I can help you, along with our entire cancer team. Why don't you tell me how the symptoms first started and what led to the diagnosis?" Trouble was, the patient didn't know he had cancer. With his jaw on his chest, he looked at me and said, "I have cancer?" Needless to say, I was shocked. So we backed up, I showed him the pathology results and the information I had, apologized that I'd seemed so blunt, and did some damage control. I didn't throw Dr. X under the bus, but said the information must have gotten crossed up somehow. Ultimately we established a very nice rapport. I took care of the patient and he has done well.

I show my respect for my patients' time by giving them as much time as they need once I'm sitting with them in the office. I want to make sure that when they leave my office, they have all the information they need, that a plan has been formulated, that they know they can call me if they have questions, and that any follow-up with me is clearly spelled out. I want them to know that their wait was worth it.

> *I don't get mad at the person in front of me at the grocery store who counts out every last nickel and dime. For all I know, he may be choosing between food and medicine.*

So how does this apply to all of us? I've learned a few things from these situations. First of all, everyone's time is valuable. My time is not more valuable than yours. I need to make every attempt to run on time so you can stay on schedule. When things change, we may not know all the extenuating circumstances. I don't get mad at the person in front of me at the grocery store who counts out every last nickel and dime. For all I know, he may be choosing between food and medicine.

Second, if you're keeping people waiting, be transparent. Let them know you're running behind. Give them options to re-schedule or to meet you later. Let them know you respect their time. Third, since you respect others' time, plan accordingly. If you have to spend time on the Internet looking for a new guitar, don't do it while others are waiting for you.

Finally, consider your response to people who keep you waiting. Do you get angry? I've learned from my own experiences that the person keeping me waiting may have a good reason. I try to give people the benefit of the doubt. If I walk out without being seen, how have I benefitted? Being angry makes me the loser. I end up being upset. It's reasonable to check with receptionists or wait staff about the delay and to make sure you've not been overlooked.

Frustration and Anger

The paragraph above made me think about anger and frustration. Prejudice is, in my estimation, a form of anger. Exploding at a team member because we have pent-up frustrations is anger.

I've realized that for me, frustration causes the anger—frustration because someone cut me off on the highway, frustration because a patient thinks I didn't do my best. What is critical is how we respond to those feelings of frustration.

When I was a kid, I loved to make plastic models of cars, airplanes, and tanks. My older cousin, also named Arthur, made car models out of die-cast metal—a lot more work. So when I was old enough and had what I thought were the skills to tackle a metal car model, I decided to make one. The pieces had to be filed, primed with paint, then painted. One day I couldn't get a piece I was screwing into the engine to fit and I began to get frustrated. I kept trying, but I couldn't do it. I could have waited for my dad to get home, but I was (and still am) way too Type A to wait. So I tried and tried. And then I blew a gasket. Angrily I picked up the first thing I could get my hands on—the hood of the car—and threw it at the stone wall of the basement. Man, that felt good. But the impact bent the hood of the car so much it looked like a fender. I reshaped it a bit, but a bend and a dent remained. I finished the model, but every time I looked at it, it reminded me of my unproductive response to frustration. I should've stepped back, used my "three-second delay," and thought before I acted.

Fast forward to now. I'm in the operating room removing a thyroid gland that is completely replaced by cancer and seems to be stuck to everything near it in the neck. I'm trying to preserve the nerves to the vocal cords, the parathyroid glands that maintain the body's calcium level, the larynx and trachea, and the carotid arteries. These cases can take hours. My own head and neck position may change very little as I focus in on a 4 x 4-cm area through 2.5x magnifying loupes (similar to what a jeweler uses). As I work I realize how stuck the gland is. I could easily get frustrated, even angry. What helps me stay calm?

I recognize the negative consequences of getting angry. I consider my strengths. I'm doing that thyroid surgery because I have experience. When you're in a difficult situation, you can use your communication skills, diplomacy, or technical skills to make a positive impact. Finally, don't be afraid to walk away.

Along with "First, do no harm," in medicine we also say "Discretion is the better part of valor." We want to make patients better without causing any harm. We want to make heroic efforts, efforts of valor, to help people, but sometimes discretion is needed to ensure that we don't harm the patient in the process.

Another term, "Peek and Shriek" applies to cases where the surgeon opens the patient, looks around ("peeks"), and sees tumor everywhere and attached to everything. There's no way to remove the cancer, so the surgeon simply closes the abdomen (and in frustration, "shrieks"). Sometimes we just have to walk away.

The patient whose neck I closed up, leaving his tumor unresected but his voice box in place, died about eight months after surgery, but he was able to speak and eat during that time. Had I removed his voice box, then discovered that the skull base tumor was unresectable, I would have done him a great disservice. In this case, walking away was in the best interest of the patient.

Respect

Teamwork, communication, time, and anger share a central theme—respect for others. Teams work well when team members respect one another. When we listen to others without interrupting, we show respect. When we acknowledge the value of each other's time, we show respect. When we respond positively to a frustrating situation, we're showing respect to those around us. Ultimately, we're showing respect for ourselves, and we're showing we're worthy of respect from others.

The ability to be introspective and willing to change is also important. We cannot change others, but we can certainly change ourselves. How do we behave on a team? How do we communicate? How do we act regarding the value of other people's time? How do we deal with frustration and anger? If we're not happy with our answers, are we willing to change? At age 10, I threw the hood across the room. At my age, I don't throw thyroids across the room. People can change.

In medical school we're conditioned to solve problems quickly, within seconds before someone else answers or before the examiner asks the next question. During my orals for my Otolaryngology board certification I wanted to answer promptly so I appeared knowledgeable. So imagine how difficult it is to sit quietly and listen without blurting out diagnoses or interrupting others. It's never too late for a little introspection and corrective action regarding our ability to work on a team, to communicate, to value others' time, and to manage frustration and anger.

Patience

When we're respectful of others and can avoid getting frustrated with them, we develop patience. Today we move quickly because we have the technology to do so. In such a fast-paced world, we need to recognize that there are times to go fast and times to go slow. We don't all move at the same pace at the same time. If we respect each other, we can be patient with each other and with ourselves. Saint Augustine wrote, "Patience is the companion of wisdom."

We need to make sure our interactions with others are enhanced, not hindered, by our use of communication technology. In short, we need to have mutual respect. What makes us rise above the Law of the Jungle is adherence to the statement, "Do unto others as you would have them do unto you." This is respect.

> *In such a fast-paced world, we need to recognize that there are times to go fast and times to go slow.*

Consider the programs and volunteer organizations that help those who are underprivileged, ill, homeless, and learning disabled. Would these exist if we didn't subscribe to "Do unto others"? We help others because we know that it's the right thing to do.

I can't speak about respect for others without citing Robert Fulghum's *All I Really Needed to Know I Learned in Kindergarten* (15th Anniversary Edition, Ballantine Books, 2003). Many of the things he learned encompass respect. Here are just a few: "Share everything; Play fair; Don't hit people; Don't take things that aren't yours; Say you're sorry when you hurt somebody."

I'm concerned about how often adults (I include myself) text one person while speaking with another, or read a magazine during a conversation (never making eye contact), or play a video game on their cell phone while speaking with the person at the checkout counter. Many of us (myself included) seem to think that the rules of respect we learned as kids don't apply to us as adults. But they do, and we shouldn't lose sight of that.

Common courtesy makes us hold the door for others. Common courtesy is the product of our belief that mutual respect should be a sacred premise and a foundation of society and our interactions with each other. With such respect, the issues regarding teamwork and communication fall nicely into place. If we act with respect towards one another, I'm confident that we can and will do the right thing.

Chapter Ten:
MORTALITY

Physicians see a significant amount of death. We accept it as part of the job. I have a lot of cancer patients, so death is present in my practice. A number of my patients have died or come close from trauma, bleeding, and airway obstruction. Time in emergency rooms has brought me-face-to face with cardiac deaths and suicides. As a result, I've made numerous observations of how we—physicians and non-physicians—deal with death or impending death, and how our attitudes toward death affect our behaviors.

> *I've made numerous observations of how we—physicians and non-physicians—deal with death or impending death, and how our attitudes toward death affect our behaviors.*

As you read the following two fictitious cases, consider your reactions and emotions. How would you feel if you read these stories in the newspaper, heard them from a friend who knew those involved, or were involved in the care or treatment of these people? Imagine one or both of these cases occurring in your own family.

CASE 1:

A 35-year-old mother of three young children is diagnosed with cervical cancer. The cancer is likely caused by HPV (Human

Papilloma Virus), a sexually transmitted virus. Her husband, a police officer, was recently killed in the line of duty, leaving her a single mother. The stress of her husband's death and the work of raising three children alone led her to neglect her own health. As a result, her cervical cancer was diagnosed at a late stage. She wants to be there for her children. But in spite of her decision to proceed with treatment, and in spite of her healthcare providers' best efforts, she dies from the disease.

CASE 2:

A 35-year-old mother of three young children is diagnosed with cervical cancer. The cancer is also likely caused by HPV from one of many sexual contacts. Her three children are from three different fathers, and she has never been married. She often uses sex to pay for her methamphetamine addiction, and her addiction has led her to neglect her health. As a result, her cervical cancer was diagnosed at a late stage. She wants to be there for her children. But in spite of her decision to proceed with treatment, and in spite of her healthcare providers' best efforts, she dies from the disease.

Do these cases affect you differently? What emotions do you feel as you read them? Consider the similarities and the differences. I haven't mentioned race, religious views, socioeconomic status, or educational background. The cancer diagnosis is a common one, and methamphetamine addiction can occur in any socioeconomic class. What details are you drawn to? Do you see the cases as very similar or very different? Is the loss in each case equal?

Many will feel sympathy for the woman in Case 1. The family suffered the loss of the father. Perhaps we feel that the woman developed cancer through no fault of her own, and if she'd been able to seek care she might have been diagnosed at an early stage.

We imagine her trying to keep her family together. Perhaps we consider how she felt going through treatment: the hair loss, the nausea and vomiting, the fatigue. We imagine how her children felt as they watched their mother die. Maybe we made assumptions about the woman's educational background and socioeconomic status.

Some will also feel pity for the woman in Case 2. But did we find ourselves judging her because she was a methamphetamine addict? Was there a sense she brought the cancer on herself? Did we assume she fed her addiction at the expense of her children? Did we feel a sense of hopelessness in her case? What assumptions did we make about her educational background and socioeconomic status?

I see both cases as tragic. A young woman passes away, leaving three children alone. Both are unable to get medical care at an early stage of disease—perhaps our medical system failed to provide adequate care, or perhaps the women lacked community support or health education so they didn't understand the risk of cervical cancer and the screening tests (Pap smear). I feel anger that in some way the system failed these women. Did they have health insurance? Was healthcare available in their communities?

Suppose we felt contempt for the woman in Case 2. But suppose she was born to abusive parents and was sexually assaulted by multiple family members. Maybe the Department of Social Services became involved and sent her into a foster home. She became pregnant at 15, lived in a halfway house for young single mothers, and dropped out of school. Over time, she found herself in and out of abusive relationships, similar to those she'd experienced as a child. She had a second child, but the father soon left. She was introduced to substances by a woman who was her one steady contact. Eventually, she turned to methamphetamine.

As her addiction worsened, she began to sell herself to support her habit and had her third child. She was diagnosed with end-stage cancer. The Department of Social Services placed her children in separate foster homes.

Do these facts change our opinion of this woman who had so many strikes against her? If we had any contempt toward her, do we now feel anger at a system that failed her?

As a surgeon and physician I regard the circumstances behind the disease as insignificant in terms of treatment (unless they somehow affect which chemotherapy, surgery, or radiation plan I choose). The circumstances are important if they can serve as a springboard to encourage education about prevention and early detection. In treating the women, I'd try to find ways to help with the family stressors they'd have during treatment, and in such advanced cases, to find ways to help their children. There is no room for judgment. It does not serve my patients, and could cloud my judgment in treating them.

Yet how often do we look at people and their circumstances and judge them by our own standards without knowing all the facts? I think our response to hearing of such tragedies is based on a very simple fact: many, if not most of us, fear our own mortality.

Many, if not most of us, fear our own mortality.

When I was 18, I worked in a local emergency room as an orderly—an amazing job. The Boston University Six-Year Medical Program had accepted me, and the doctors and nurses at the hospital liked me and gave me a lot of responsibilities. I usually worked the night shift, so we saw a lot of real emergencies—motor vehicle accidents, heart attacks, airway problems, and so on. One of my jobs was performing chest compressions on cardiac arrest victims ("code blue" situations). Most of the codes involved elderly people or patients with severe cardiac histories. Most of these patients did not make it.

One day during Christmas vacation we received an ambulance call. The paramedics were bringing in a man in full cardiac arrest. When they arrived, they moved the patient into Room One, ventilating him with an Ambu bag and providing chest compressions. I took over giving compressions. The ER doctor intubated the patient. His clothes were cut away to give access to place intravenous lines. One of the cardiologists came down to assist, and we worked on that patient for over two hours (a long time for a code blue) but we couldn't resuscitate him, and eventually he was pronounced dead.

I don't remember his name. But I remember his face, and the winter coat he wore, because we cut parts of it away to get intravenous access. And I remember every muscle in my body hurting as I provided chest compressions. I remember the cardiologist saying to me, "If this guy makes it, he owes you dinner." I particularly remember the screams of his wife when the emergency room doctor told her that her husband had apparently collapsed on the street in full cardiac arrest and had died. I remember her screaming that it was not true, that it couldn't be true, that he couldn't be gone. I remember all of this because I remember that he was 27 years old—that's right, 27 years old!

I remember this case because I looked for the answers we all look for. At that moment I realized how much I feared my own mortality. This guy was only nine years older than I was. I wanted to find out that he smoked two packs per day. But he was a non-smoker. I wanted to learn he had a substance abuse history like cocaine that caused him to be at risk for sudden cardiac death. But he didn't. I wanted to find out that he'd fallen on the ice and had struck his head, causing a brainstem injury or some other intracranial event leading to a cardiac event. But you guessed it—he had no head trauma. None of the doctors and nurses could explain his death.

I became acutely aware of my own mortality and realized how quickly and unexpectedly death can occur. The guy who had just been pronounced dead could be me! Did I lose sleep over that? You bet! I'm in my late 50s now and I remember that day as if it were yesterday.

I share this true story because I think it explains our responses to hearing about death. When we hear that someone has died an "untimely death," it's human nature to look at the circumstances and try to rationalize that death. We want to feel some control over our own mortality. We want to reassure ourselves that it won't happen to us, or learn how we can avoid the situations that led to that death. One of the Three Stooges, in an episode in which they faced execution, was asked what manner of death he wanted. He replied, "Old age."

Do you read the obituaries? I do. I guess it's part of getting older. I use the excuse that I might learn that a patient of mine in hospice for end-stage cancer has passed away, and want to send condolences. I find myself checking the ages of those who've passed away. When I read the obituary of an 88-year-old, I think, "God bless her," yet when I see the obituary of a 50-year-old, I sigh with fear and exasperation. I want to know if he died after a long illness, or whether donations are being made to hospice, or to some foundation for chronic illness. It frightens me when I see "died suddenly." I also try to figure out if this young person passed away from something I can avoid (maybe climbing Mount Everest!). Again, I try to rationalize it.

Is there anything good to take from this? We can agree to withhold judgment when we see someone suffering from a terrible illness, even if we believe past behavior has somehow contributed to that illness. If we put our judgments aside, we can move more quickly to compassion and empathy, and then work to help such a person. We can accept the responsibility for caring for others in need. Some very special people are moved by compassion and empathy to volunteer at cancer centers and hospice facilities. Others help with donations of money or time, putting together books, gifts, or food.

Road Rage and Compassion

Consider this. You're driving along on the highway, and someone on a motorcycle or in a tiny sports car passes you at 90 miles an hour. Perhaps you thought, "That maniac is on the way to an accident. He deserves what he gets." Did you really mean it? Of course not. You were expressing fear of your own mortality and, therefore, making an attempt to control your own destiny. If I don't speed or drive recklessly, I won't be putting myself in danger like that guy.

Suppose your attitude toward someone who cuts you off is, "Hey, maybe he's on his way to an emergency," rather than, "I'll show that jerk; I'm going to speed up and cut him off!" One night the ER called about a patient with a severe nosebleed who might bleed to death. I raced to the hospital, but two blocks from the hospital, I got behind a car that was driving below the speed limit. I tried to pass him, thinking that every second counted. I was definitely tailgating him. A pickup truck pulled up next to me and the driver screamed at me for tailgating. He even tried to push me off the road.

I was wearing my scrubs and lab coat, but it was too dark for the driver to notice. I was wrong for tailgating, but my mind was focused on getting to the hospital to save a life. I made it in time.

What if the pickup truck had driven me off the road and I arrived at the ER too late to save the patient? People exsanguinate from severe nosebleeds, so this isn't farfetched. What did the driver gain? Did he feel he was upholding justice? What if he'd known that I'd recorded his license plate number. If the patient had died and I'd had to explain my delay, I would describe exactly what happened and who tried to drive me off the road.

Would confronting the truck driver have accomplished anything? Given my second-degree black belt in Kyuso-Kempo karate, I'm not afraid of having to physically defend myself. But a confrontation would've delayed me. And suppose the truck driver had been injured by someone who'd tailgated him.

The point is that there are so many sides to the stories we hear, it's impossible to make a judgment. Rather, let us act out of compassion and empathy.

Fear of Vulnerability

Fearing our mortality is linked to our fear of vulnerability. When we hear about a crime, disaster, or catastrophe, we think that could have been me. Perhaps a plane crash occurred on a flight we've taken in the past.

I'm bothered when I read of a sexual assault—a woman abducted while jogging—and someone says, "She shouldn't have been out jogging alone." That places blame on the victim.

In a perfect world, we should be able to move about freely without fear of being assaulted or raped. These are crimes of violence, not of sexual desire. So why would we blame the victim? Doing so may make us feel less vulnerable and more in control. We're explaining why the crime occurred so we can assure ourselves that such a crime could never happen to us. The problem is that such rationalizing statements carry judgment, which can border on prejudice. The blame game, the holier-than-thou mindset may make us feel less vulnerable, but it's not productive or constructive.

Prejudice leads cultures to enslave each other, religions to attack each other, and races to slaughter each other. Behind oppression is prejudice, fear, and vulnerability. Now consider the work of healthcare providers, EMT workers, firefighters, and police officers.

> *Awareness of our common vulnerability and mortality can help us respect each other.*

They don't freeze up or fail to perform because they fear their own mortality. There is no room for prejudice. They don't let judgment affect their performance.

Awareness of our common vulnerability and mortality can help us respect each other. When we're compassionate, not judgmental, we can do the right thing.

ARTHUR LAURETANO

140

Chapter Eleven:
SUCCESS

Are you successful? Am I successful? Think about these questions for a moment. Now let me rephrase them. Do you think you're successful? Do I think I'm successful? Note the difference between the questions "Am I successful?" and "Do *I think* I am successful?"

In this chapter, I discuss defining success. It won't surprise you that I think the definition is relative. We must define success *for ourselves*, not based on how others define it. We may redefine success to

> *Note the difference between the questions "Am I successful?" and "Do* I think *I am successful?"*

make a goal more realistic, or after we've reached a goal, or maybe conditions have changed. This does not mean we've failed. In fact, I encourage redefining success.

An Example from Surgery

I'll start with a case from my surgical practice that spanned a few years. Mr. Q was a former smoker and came to me with a large lump in his neck that had been present for several months. It was getting larger and had not improved with antibiotics. My immediate concern was that the lump was a cancer related to his smoking history. Usually such neck masses are lymph nodes containing cancer cells that have spread from an initial (or primary) cancer somewhere in the throat. So I looked for a source but couldn't find one. I performed a needle biopsy of the neck lump and it proved to be squamous cell carcinoma (cancer), the most common type of cancer we see in the head and neck, particularly in smokers. As I didn't find the primary cancer I considered him to have a squamous cell cancer of the neck with an unknown primary. The size of his neck mass and the status of his cancer as an unknown primary made him a candidate for one of our chemotherapy/radiation protocols. His neck node didn't require surgery according to this protocol unless the node persisted in spite of the chemotherapy and radiation. So he underwent the seven weeks of chemotherapy and radiation. He had a complete response, meaning that the cancer was completely gone. And he continued to do well.

We'd consider this a success, correct? He had cancer and we resolved it. However, about 18 months later, the tumor started to grow back in his neck in the same spot. He'd had maximal radiation to the neck, so the only option was to proceed with surgery. We did a neck dissection and removed the entire tumor. He healed well after the surgery with normal neck function except for some expected weakness in the shoulder on the operated side (a nerve in that neck that goes to the shoulder has to be removed if it's involved in the cancer). He was able to eat and drink normally and returned to work.

We were successful again, correct? But three years later the tumor grew back in the same side of the neck, with nodules in the lungs proven to be metastatic cancer to the lung. That is, the original neck cancer had grown back in the neck and had sent off satellite cells that nested and were growing in the lungs. At this point, surgery would not cure the disease. The neck could not benefit from more surgery because the tumor encased the carotid artery. Removing this artery has significant risks and the long-term benefit from a cancer standpoint is marginal. Also, this would not impact the lung disease. Radiation was not an option. That left chemotherapy to keep the cancer in check, slow its growth and progression, and give the patient maximum time before he succumbed to the cancer.

Did we consider this a failure? In spite of all of our efforts, the cancer kept returning and was now in the lungs. We exhausted treatment options except for very aggressive ones with considerable side effects. He decided against those and asked to be kept comfortable. He died peacefully without pain, with his family nearby.

Success? Failure? His original cancer had a fair prognosis at best. The recurrences were not a surprise. Even under these circumstances, when a patient dies, I feel a sense of failure, wishing I could've done more. But was the case overall a failure? Remember the quote from William Osler, M.D.: "The good physician treats the disease; the great physician treats the patient who has the disease."

This patient knew his disease was advanced. Yet my team and I were optimistic about a cure. He had a complete response to his initial chemotherapy and radiation, so I felt we were on the right track. Even when the cancer came back I was still optimistic. A cancer that comes back in spite of chemotherapy and radiation is by definition a more aggressive cancer. So it wasn't a surprise that his cancer came back after surgery. But I'd still been optimistic. I mention this because, throughout all the treatment, Mr. Q was realistic in his expectations. When the recurrences were diagnosed, he was disappointed but not surprised. He accepted the diagnosis, and weighed the options. He made it clear that he didn't see any of the treatments as failures because in every case we'd prolonged his life.

This outlook was refreshing. Mr. Q. did something I find difficult. He redefined his goals. By redefining his goals, he redefined his definition of success. He defined success on his own terms.

Success or failure? When Mr. Q. knew he was going to die and changed the discussion from "If I die" to "When I die," he set aside the goal of surviving. He set new goals—walking one of his daughters down the aisle on her wedding day, and seeing another daughter give birth to his first grandchild. For the six months before these events we kept the cancer in check with chemotherapy and controlled the side effects. He walked his daughter down the aisle and a few weeks later, his first grandchild—a boy—was born. Two months after that, when the side effects of chemotherapy outweighed the benefits, he decided to stop treatment. He died about a month later.

Success means different things to each of us. We cannot let others impose their definition of success on us.

I learned from Mr. Q. that success is relative. When I treat cancer patients, I want to cure them. Some die. And I still wonder whether we could have tried yet another technique. I have to realize that in some cases the goals need to change. An observer might say of Mr. Q., "How could that be a success? He died from his cancer." Mr. Q. might reply, "It was a success. I'm satisfied because I accomplished my goals." Success means different things to each of us. We cannot let others impose their definition of success on us.

Redefining Goals

During my senior year of medical school, I interviewed at many places for otolaryngology residencies (ENT training). My goal was to do a five-year ENT residency and take an academic position where I could treat patients, do very complicated surgeries, teach residents, and conduct research. At a program in Virginia, the department chair reviewed my plans and asked whether I saw myself in charge of a department. I'd never given it much thought. But he encouraged me to become an academic ENT surgeon and to set a goal to chair an ENT department, or at least contribute in a big way to the academic field of otolaryngology. I did my residency in Boston at Massachusetts Eye and Ear Infirmary/Harvard Medical School, and pursued my interest in an academic position. After residency, I took an academic position where I did complicated surgery, treating patients with ENT problems that fascinated me; taught students and residents; and conducted research. I hoped to gain the experience, expertise, and credentials that would make me a "heavy hitter" in the academic world of ENT. This was my definition of success.

But life had other plans for me. The situation at home I mentioned earlier made it impossible to balance my ideal academic career and my responsibilities at home. I had to make a hard choice. I chose to leave the full-time academic world and go into private practice. I still teach and do complicated surgeries, but in a community location, sometimes taking cases to larger academic centers.

Initially I questioned myself. Was this failure? Occasionally, when I see a contemporary who stayed in academia, I think, "I could have been a full-time academic and made a major impact in my field." If I persisted in defining success that way, I'd indeed have to admit failure.

Many people fed into this and said I was wasting my talents. Some accused me of wanting more money. Those who had "high hopes" for me were disappointed. They saw my move to the community as a step down—in short, a failure.

Fast forward to today. Our practice performs high-level care in a community setting. Patients don't have to travel long distances, and we pride ourselves on doing many tertiary-level (third-level) cases. I'm president of the medical staff and medical director of our multidisciplinary head and neck cancer center. I lecture to medical students yearly, to the medical staff at community hospitals, to community patient groups, and at local high schools on smoking cessation. I do all this and have more time at home with my family.

I set new goals and redefined success for myself. When I reached some goals, I set new ones within the framework of a community hospital. As president of the medical staff, I learn about the hospital from a different perspective and contribute to our medical community and the local community around the hospital in ways I'd not envisioned. At some point, I may get an MBA or an MPH (Masters of Public Health) to find new ways to contribute to medicine, particularly in our community. One new opportunity opens doors to others.

> *When we're happy, we perform better; when we perform better, we're happy.*

I'm fascinated by people who reach what looks like an ultimate goal (winning a prestigious award or making a critical scientific discovery) then set a new goal. These highly motivated people are happy but not complacent. The work ethic that enabled their success drives them to seek new ways to make things better, more efficient, or more productive. They continue to set new goals and continue to strive for new successes.

I'm not saying we shouldn't shoot for the stars. But it's wise to mix in a dose of realism and have a fallback plan. If you applied to college, you probably had a few "safe schools" you knew would accept you, and had other schools that were higher on your list. Then you had the "reach schools" that were a bit of a stretch. You applied to a variety. You weren't complacent. You had high hopes. And you were realistic.

I wanted to be a professional guitar player at one point, but a career in medicine was more realistic, so I redefined my goals in guitar playing. With graying hair and an expanding waistline, I doubt I'll become the next guitar god. I'd describe myself as a "wannabe in a has-been's body." But that won't stop me from possibly taking courses at Berklee College of Music in Boston to learn more about guitar playing, recording, or some other facet of music. And I can have success as long as the goals I set and my definitions of success are reasonable.

Sometimes others define your success. Olympic gymnasts' scores depend on the judges' opinions. But the gymnasts still control their destiny by doing their best. Artists' works are critiqued by others, but they put forth the work they think is their best. The issue is not "Do they like it?" but "Do you like it?"

Your family and friends wanted you to be a doctor or a lawyer, but you wanted to teach third grade. Each June, you know your class is moving on to fourth grade with experiences you provided. When September comes, you're excited about teaching a new group of students. Success or failure?

Success is tied to happiness. People are happy when they've achieved success that they, not others, have defined.

Consider this case. A CEO wants his company to be the top-seller of a medical device. He's made billions of dollars, been featured in business magazines on turning around failing companies, diversifying into international markets—you name it. But he can't bring his company beyond second place. By many definitions of success, he's a successful man. But he's not happy because he sees himself as a failure.

If our goals are too lofty, we may never reach them, never see ourselves as a success, and may never be happy. This CEO could redefine the company as the top seller for a certain product line, or within a specific geographic region, or recognize that being second is still pretty darn good. When we're happy, we perform better; when we perform better, we're happy. When we're successful and happy, doing our work honestly and with the good of others in mind, we're doing the right thing.

My dad's career provides another view of success. When I was a kid, my parents considered college a necessity so I could have a respectable profession (architect, doctor, engineer, lawyer, etc.). Neither of my parents has a college degree. They graduated high school in the late 1950s. At that time, going to college was a big deal. In the eyes of my parents and their contemporaries, having their kids go to college was a goal because they didn't achieve it themselves.

During my childhood, I felt that my father saw himself, to some extent, as a failure because he didn't go to college (I apologize to my dad if I'm wrong). My going to college was in some way an opportunity to reach a goal he'd never achieved, and he hoped I'd have an easier life as a result. He might have defined success this way: "I didn't go to college, but my son is graduating from college, and now I'm successful because I was able to put him through college." When I came off the stage at Boston University with my undergraduate and medical school diplomas in hand, the first person I hugged was my dad. In that moment, his smile told me he felt as if he'd also graduated college.

Look at my dad's career. About one month before he was born, his father died of pulmonary disease. He grew up in a second-floor apartment with his mother, who worked as a seamstress, and five sisters, and a brother who soon left for the military. They shared a bathroom down the hall with all the tenants on the second floor. When he was little, his sisters bathed him in the kitchen sink. He wasn't a good student. He grew up in Boston's North End (as did my mom) where rivalries existed between groups of kids from different streets, and my dad got into his share of trouble. A Jesuit priest named Father William Ott guided my father and probably kept him from getting into even more trouble.

> *Reaching for new goals enables people to invent and discover, make an impact on society, and do the right thing.*

My dad boxed and played high-school and semi-professional football. Getting through high school was a struggle, but he graduated from Christopher Columbus High School. He took courses at Wentworth Institute of Technology in Boston for general engineering, but didn't get a degree. He has worked as a carpenter, a carpenter's foreman, a superintendent, a general superintendent/project manager, and vice president and senior vice president, and has overseen such projects as major hospitals and colleges in the Greater Boston area and in New England. He was appointed to the Barr & Barr Board of Directors in 2004. He took classes at the Harvard School of Public Health in "Guidelines for Laboratory Design" and at Tufts University in "Procedures and Practices for Asbestos Abatement." He has a builder's license and a real-estate license. He's a member of the Construction Management, Industrial and Professional Advisory Committee (IPAC) at Wentworth Institute of Technology and a member of the St. Ann's Home Board of Directors (a home for children with educational and psychological problems in Methuen, Mass). Add in his community service projects: cub master when I was a cub scout, volunteer for the Medford string organization when I played violin and bass, Holy Name Society president, and current member of the Finance and Building Committee at St. Francis Church. And he's a great dad!

Is my dad a success? In my eyes, he always was. But in his eyes, not until I graduated college. Once I did that, he set his sights on new goals and defined new successes. My point here is that success is relative. For my father, it was about my graduating college, in spite of all the great things he accomplished. Most important, his definition of success was his own.

People often equate wealth with success. My concern is whether they're measuring their worth by what others think of them. Many who think that way are insecure because they've tied their self-worth and self-respect to how others view them. I question how happy they are. If you come across as seeking wealth at all costs, especially if you're motivated by impressing others, you may actually be yearning for self-respect.

Wealth is relative. It differs for each of us. Your wealth may be financial, the family that surrounds you, your health, or the pleasure you get from helping others. Our definitions of wealth have something in common with our definitions of success— they're all relative and we must define them for ourselves.

Success is not guaranteed, even when we've defined it for ourselves. When we don't meet our goals we reassess, redefine, or alter our approach. What we define as success today may need to be redefined tomorrow. Reaching for new goals enables people to invent and discover, make an impact on society, and do the right thing.

I've read many books on success and achievement and many surgical books on techniques for getting better outcomes with surgical procedures. For the administrative side of my practice I read Jim Collins' *Good to Great* (2001, William Collins Publishing), *Built to Last* (2002, HarperCollins), Dale Carnegie's *How to Win Friends and Influence People* (1936, Simon and Schuster), Stephen Covey's *The 7 Habits of Highly Effective People* (1989, Free Press), *The 8th Habit* (2004, Free Press) and Peter Drucker's *Management: Revised Edition* (2008, HarperCollins). Books like *The Secret*, by Rhonda Byrne (2006, Beyond Words Publishing) and Eckhart Tolle's *The Power of Now* (1999, New World Library) can be inspirational. I've learned a lot from my reading—ways to improve myself, my practice, my relationships, and my outlook on life.

Dr. Seuss on Success

One book sums up what it means to achieve success, and what it means to experience failure. This book addresses you and takes you through our common peaks and valleys. The author of this book is none other than Theodor Seuss Geisel—that's right, Dr. Seuss—and the book is *Oh, the Places You'll Go!* (1990, Random House).

This is his last book. Before you close my book thinking I'm some kind of nut, read it. Already read it? Please read it again. I've read it to my kids every year at the end of the school year since my daughter finished kindergarten. Dr. Seuss presents an astute perspective on understanding life's ups and downs. You can read it in 15 minutes, or you can contemplate each page, applying the ideas to your own life.

The book appeals to me because it focuses on you, just as success should be defined by you and for you. Dr. Seuss tells us, "You're off to Great Places!... You're on your own. And you know what you know. And YOU are the guy who'll decide where to go."

The book is positive—many choices and opportunities lie ahead, and if you look up and down the streets of your town, and don't see places you'd choose, then "you'll head straight out of town" where it is "opener" and where "things can happen." "You'll start happening too. OH! THE PLACES YOU'LL GO."

> *Acknowledge the silent successes only you can appreciate. They matter just as much.*

The book is also realistic. Dr. Seuss tells us that "Wherever you go, you will top all the rest. Except when you don't. Because, sometimes, you won't." We can turn failures into successes. "He who fails to learn from history is doomed to repeat it," says the Spanish philosopher George Santayana (the quote has also been attributed to Winston Churchill). I remember the test questions I got wrong as a student far better than those I got right. They prompted me to review the material so I'd never make the same mistake again. According to Dr. Seuss, our life experiences teach us that "Bang-ups and Hang-ups can happen to you."

I love Dr. Seuss's "The Waiting Place." He describes it as "a most useless place" where we can end up when we're in a "slump," when we aren't reaching our goals or even on the path to them. I read this to say there are times things won't go well, and our vision of success seems out of reach. We can't wait for something to come along and help us. We need to act, look at our goals and our approaches to them, and redefine them. Then look for the opportunity that will allow us to achieve that success.

Becoming an ENT surgeon took four years of medical school and five years of residency. We need to pay dues and learn lessons. I've talked about redefining fairness, reevaluating teams, and moving on. This may take weeks, months, years. Meanwhile, we keep working to improve ourselves and creating opportunities. And if we're in "The Waiting Place" because we've been overlooked or because we feel someone else has wronged us, keep moving. As Dr. Seuss says, escape "all that waiting and staying. You'll find the bright places where Boom Bands are playing."

Dr. Seuss says "some times you'll play lonely games too. Games you can't win 'cause you'll play against you." I've achieved seemingly small personal successes, doing something better than before. Maybe in surgery I used a subtle technique others didn't notice to avert a complication. This success that I've defined accrues to my goal that my patient wakes up and every nerve and muscle is working. There won't be any medals or awards for that move. Acknowledge the silent successes only you can appreciate. They matter just as much.

The message in *Oh, the Places You'll Go!* is timeless. It's about you. In spite of all challenges and setbacks, we need to "Step with care and great tact and remember that Life's a Great Balancing Act .... be dexterous and deft. And never mix up your right foot with your left."

In other words *do the right thing.* "And will you succeed? Yes! You will, indeed! (98 and 3/4 percent guaranteed.) *KID, YOU'LL MOVE MOUNTAINS!*" How positive is that! Success is about you because you've defined it.

ARTHUR LAURETANO

Learning From Failure

Look at your career as a professional, as part of a household, as a volunteer. In any framework we have highs and lows. Are you learning from your failures?

How do you deal with failure? I know people with what I call the "Wile E. Coyote Approach." Wile E. Coyote was Warner Brothers' genius coyote who continually tried to catch the Roadrunner. He tried all kinds of brilliant schemes, often using equipment he got from ACME. I know I sound like a geek, but as a kid, I could never understand why, when one of his ideas failed, he didn't go back and tweak it and try again. Instead, he abandoned the idea and tried something completely different. I know people who approach their goals the same way. I'd say they've lost and lost the lesson. Some people, rather than fail again, drop the whole idea.

Others try the same approach over and over again, expecting a different outcome. Maybe they blame conditions or luck or other people. Albert Einstein's definition of insanity is "doing the same thing over and over again and expecting different results." I hope we fall somewhere in the middle.

I applied the lessons in *Oh, the Places You'll Go!* when I had to balance the demands of work with those at home. Something had to change. Plenty of people were willing to help, but I needed to figure out what worked best for me. I found myself in "The Waiting Place," waiting for something, someone to come along and make things right. But I needed to do that for myself.

At that time, success meant giving up the idea of being a full-time academician so I could be home more often. It meant moving into a community practice. I was uncertain. I sometimes felt the good things I was doing in medicine were going unnoticed because I wasn't doing them in a big academic center. Finally, I concluded

I could "move mountains," smaller ones in a community I love to serve, in hospitals that pride themselves on giving the best medical care. Success meant having a positive impact on that community.

I can apply these ideas to a single year of fatherhood. The day my son was born, there was great joy in our family. Yet four months later, he had a feeding tube and his stomach completely shut down, possibly related to a vaccination. Then came all the low points: the exhaustion, sleeplessness, questioning faith. All that created tension in our family. *Would he survive?* How would we tell our daughter that her new brother was going to die? Then, six months after the tube went in, once the little guy was stable on his tube feedings, his stomach began to gain some function. New challenges cropped up:: pneumonia (and a near respiratory arrest) and learning disabilities possibly related to the initial illness. But we got past them and came out the other side to a new high point.

As parents we have visions: what it's like to be a parent, how our kids will be, what they'll be good at, and where they'll struggle. Things can change. Our vision of a healthy child turns into the reality of caring for a child with an illness, or making the best of a child's short time on earth.

In the chapter on impact, I asked you to have your George Bailey moment. Now I want you to look at the successes you've defined for yourself. In the summer of 1984, I was finishing my undergraduate courses at the Boston University Six-year Medical Program. I took a class called "Death and Dying." We looked at different views of death in different cultures. We read Elisabeth Kubler-Ross' ground-breaking work, *On Death and Dying* (1969, Routledge), that describes the "Five Stages of Grief." An exercise that stands out to this day was our homework assignment to write our own obituary. Usually someone else writes your obituary (some do their own in advance). She asked us to look at the positive things we'd done, the accomplishments we were proud of, and the ways we wanted to be remembered.

My Challenges to You

So, you guessed it. I want you to write your own obituary. Suppose, as a doctor, I tell you through my magic crystal ball, that you'll die in five days. In your obituary you want people to know everything about you: your life, your personality, your interests. You have unlimited space in the local paper. Go wild. Write about everything that is good: every interest, every positive impact, every success, no matter how small. Include the obvious ones, such as beloved husband or devoted mother, but go into detail. Chair of the XYZ company, dedicated to co-workers. Everyone loved his jokes. Did a great Groucho Marx impersonation. Adored Dr. Seuss. Loved to build Lego models with her daughter. Took pleasure in the smiles of senior citizens at the nursing home where every Friday she read stories.

Maybe future generations will read it. Maybe your family will learn things they didn't know.

Now, here comes a curve ball. Finish the obituary, read it over a few times, and make sure you didn't miss anything. (Remember that cool trophy when your little league team won the local baseball tournament? Put that down.) Then (this is only for you) make a list of your regrets, the things you wish you'd done differently, or wish you'd done. (Remember, in this scenario you have five more days to live so you might not get to cross them off.) List the times you had a negative impact or didn't act when you should have. Did you hurt or mistreat someone? Look far back and in deep. This is between you and you, so be honest.

The third list I want you to make is your "bucket list," the things you always wanted to do before you "kick the bucket." (Someone once asked me what was on my bucket list. I said, "Buy a bucket.") Now let's say that I, your doctor, tell you there's a pill that will extend your five days to six months. You have all that time to do what's on your bucket list. Now let's say you have unlimited funds and for those six months you'll be fit as a fiddle. So go ahead and make the list. Maybe you want to see a concert, or donate time to an organization you admire, or visit a far-off paradise. Maybe you want to go fishing with your grandchildren every Saturday, or play your guitar at a local blues club. Include everything!

> *When we consider regrets, we may think of material things or trips, but overlook the complex issues of relationships or times we've made mistakes.*

Finished with the obituary, the list of regrets, and the bucket list? Good.

Now, put the lists in front of you: regrets on the left, bucket list in the middle, obituary on the right. Go down the regret list. Suppose a regret is "Wish I had gone to Fiji." Now look at the bucket list. Does it say "Travel to Fiji"? Now assume you do travel to Fiji. You could add a new line to your obituary: "Visited Fiji." Understand my thought process? Consider another regret: "Wanted to run a marathon." Bucket list: "Run the Boston Marathon." Obit: "Ran the Boston Marathon in her last six months of life." How does that feel?

Next step. Suppose your regret list read: "I regret not speaking to my sister for the last 15 years because of a foolish family argument." Does your bucket list say "Call my sister and patch up our relationship"? Can you add to your obituary: "Settled a longstanding disagreement with family"?

When we consider regrets, we may think of material things or trips, but overlook the complex issues of relationships or times we've made mistakes. What if we periodically took stock of our lives and made the three lists above? What if we periodically assessed ourselves, our accomplishments, and the good we've done, as well as the chances we have to mend fences and resolve regrets?

On the TV comedy My Name is Earl (2005-2009) we see an example of righting wrongs. Jason Lee played Earl Hickey, who had a list of the bad things he'd done and vowed, one by one, to make things right. Each episode showed his attempts to right at least one thing. There were many comedic moments. Earl's regret list became his bucket list.

Do we try to fix things often enough or turn our regrets into accomplishments? Not every regret can be fixed. Perhaps you tried and were rebuffed. Sometimes the damage can't be repaired. Arguments with colleagues or family fights seem to get worse over time. Waiting for heads to cool is a good idea, but letting things fester can keep things on the regret list. If we want to minimize our regrets, it helps to assess our selves and our successes, failures, and regrets, frequently and honestly.

Managing Success

Being successful doesn't mean we don't ask for help. One of the great things about medicine is the endless opportunity to share medical knowledge and gain from the expertise of colleagues. Remember the instruction from my residency days, "Feel free to call, but remember, calling is a sign of weakness"? Asking for help shows humility. You know your limitations, when to refer to someone with more expertise. It also shows good judgment and the self-confidence of knowing it's fine to bring others in to solve a problem or achieve success. The greatest failure is being afraid to try.

On the opposite end of the spectrum are the words attributed to Nelson Mandela: "Our deepest fear is not that we are inadequate. Our deepest fear is that we are powerful beyond measure." Maybe we fear success because we don't know how to handle it or think it was just luck, and if the situation were to recur, we would never be able to recreate it.

My last point it this. Celebrate your successes, large and small. Too often we rush on to the next goal. To quote the old cliché, "Stop and smell the roses." They're your accomplishments and deserve celebration. And remember to define success on your own terms.

> *The greatest failure is being afraid to try.*

Dale Carnegie said, "Success is getting what you want. Happiness is wanting what you get." When we define success for ourselves, I believe we can be both happy and successful. When we strive for such success with honesty, faith in our abilities, and concern for others, with each effort we do the right thing.

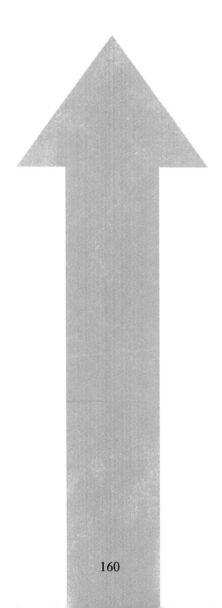

Chapter Twelve:
TEACHING, LEARNING, AND YOUR LEGACY

When I planned this book, I thought "Success and Failure" would be my last chapter, followed by "Closing Thoughts." I also wanted to say something about teaching and passing on what we've learned. As I finished chapter after chapter, I couldn't decide where to put the chapter on teaching. Many of my thoughts on teaching were based on the ideas in the chapter on success, because when we achieve success, our work is not done. We have an obligation to show succeeding generations what has succeeded and what has failed. This is our legacy.

In medicine we have many great teachers: our professors and instructors in medical school and the practicing physicians during internship and residency, where a lot of training is on the job. As a surgeon, a lot of my training was in the operating room, working side-by-side with an attending surgeon, and in some cases, a more senior resident. When we began training in the operating room, we observed procedures and sometimes held retractors to help the main surgeons. As time went on we became part of the surgical team while still medical students, interns, or residents. We cut some sutures once they're placed, then did the suturing. Later, we got to make incisions, then do some dissection. Eventually, we performed the entire surgery under the close guidance of the attendings. This was how we learned to perform procedures by ourselves.

We learned some procedures early, so that at the end of the first or second year of residency we could place ear tubes, remove small skin lesions, perform tonsillectomies and adenoidectomies, and so on. During ENT residency in our middle years we learned sinus surgery, and in our senior years performed complicated head, neck, and ear surgeries. By the end of residency, we had a number of procedures under our belt. We may have needed extra training for some procedures—a fellowship, or working with a more senior surgeon. Over time, maybe we wanted to brush up on some procedure, or new techniques were developed, and we took courses. Medicine is full of teaching and learning opportunities.

Teaching and learning in medicine depend on people being available to teach, and that means more than passing on knowledge. Our teachers wanted us to question it, add to it, correct it, and improve on it. They passed it on in hopes we'd make medicine better. Our teachers were unselfish. They allowed us to operate with them on their own patients, taking more time than if they'd done it alone. They treated us as associates. I remember doing procedures on patients who received local anesthesia so were awake, and the attending made it clear that I, the resident, was going to do most of the procedure.

> *One of my mentors said you didn't truly know a procedure until you could teach it to someone else.*

These clinicians saw the benefits of showing students how to do something, then seeing them perform that same task. One of my mentors said you didn't truly know a procedure until you could teach it to someone else.

What fascinates me about teachers is they understand they're passing on knowledge future generations will use. That knowledge is their legacy. They impart what they've learned so we can avoid their mistakes, make our own mark on medicine, then pass it on.

Many great medical innovations and technologies are based on concepts that were introduced 100 to 200 years ago.

Mentors

If you taught your kid to tie his shoe, you passed on something you learned. Or you taught your daughter to drive. Maybe you volunteered at a school and taught a tradition from your family or ethnic background. Our advances as a society depend on our predecessors sharing their knowledge with the generations that followed them.

While I was thinking about this chapter, I received my copy of *Pharos*, the publication from the Alpha Omega Alpha Medical Honor Society. The editorial "Mentoring and coaching in medicine" by Richard L. Byyny, M.D. in the 2012 winter edition echoed my thoughts. Dr. Byyny notes that in Homer's *Odyssey*. the character Mentor was the "wise and trusted counselor." Dr. Byyny explains, "Physicians can be excellent mentors because of their motivation to serve, to share knowledge and experience, and their commitment to caring." The mentor, or teacher, works, he says, "to guarantee a protégé's success." *Guarantee!* That's awesome— you're making sure that your trainee, your student, your *mentee* gets it and successfully applies it.

It probably doesn't surprise you that I love to teach. When my student gets it, I know I've made sense. When I see my student apply what I've taught and help a patient, I know I've had a positive impact on someone through the hands of another. You could call this a vicarious positive impact. And when I teach multiple people, the positive effect can be exponential.

ARTHUR LAURETANO

Quitting

In my first year of ENT residency I worked with attending surgeon Dr. Jo Shapiro, who later became a colleague in academic practice in Boston. Jo still is one of the best, most empathetic teachers I've ever had. She understands the ups and downs of being a resident or a medical student. She does incredible work for students and residents at Harvard Medical School, and is Chief of the Division of Otolaryngology at Boston's Brigham and Woman's Hospital.

I was scrubbing for a case and Dr. Shapiro leaned over to me and said, "So, are you ready to quit yet?" I remember thinking, "Oh my God, she knows how beaten I feel, how miserable I am right now." This was the middle of winter, I was on call every other night, trudging through snow from the emergency room at one hospital to the emergency room at another. I spent most of my time in clinics and seeing emergency consults. I constantly compared this to my first postgraduate year when I operated quite a bit as an intern in general surgery. I'd considered going back to general surgery because my colleagues were performing a lot of operations. Also I'd been asked to forego the ENT residency and stay in general surgery.

So when Jo asked me that, I figured everyone knew I was miserable and I'd probably be fired. But instead she said, "I'm asking you because when I was in your shoes, I was ready to quit also." This is a mentor's empathy. Then she explained that once I got through the first year of ENT residency, I'd operate a lot and be very happy. She was right. That information was part of her legacy.

That legacy continued as I passed that information on to residents I trained. They were on the brink of quitting because they'd lost confidence or weren't sure they'd made the correct career choice. I helped them when they were struggling. They've since gone on to successful careers. They were grateful to me, and I was grateful to them, because I was among those who played a role in their progress.

In his editorial Dr. Byyny defines teaching, coaching, and mentoring with respect to personal and professional development this way:

- Teaching is "to cause one to know something, to know how, to guide the studies, to impart knowledge, to instruct by precept, example, or experience."

- A coach is "a private tutor who instructs and/or trains players, athletes, musicians in the fundamentals, skills and intricacies to improve performance."

- A mentor is "a trusted counselor guiding the professional development of an individual."

These functions overlap, and "good mentors are all of these things."

I'm going to simplify things and use the terms *teacher*, *coach* and *mentor* interchangeably. We all have opportunities to be teachers, coaches and mentors. We may teach our own families or be Big Brothers or Big Sisters in a program for underprivileged kids. We may coach a team or teach music. We may be professional or volunteer teachers. Your kids bring some friends home from school and you bake cookies with them. The kids tell their parents you taught them to make cookies.

I loved my teachers' unselfishness. They shared their knowledge freely, never fearing we'd become better surgeons. I can't tell you how many times former students have come back and shown me a new technique that improved on something I'd taught them.

Near the end of my last year of residency, at the University of Iowa Head and Neck Course, I learned a new approach to cancers at the base of the tongue, an area that previously had required splitting the jaw in the middle at the chin to gain access to the tumor. This technique meant we could avoid cutting the jaw by reaching the base of the tongue through the neck. This hastened the patient's recovery. At Mass. Eye and Ear I asked if I could use this approach on the next base-of-tongue cancer case. We did, and it worked well. This was possible thanks to the unselfishness of my teachers. I learned, the residents learned, and patients benefited.

> *When you make your ideas available to others, you haven't lost anything. Instead, you've made a contribution and have solidified your legacy.*

There may be times when you want to keep a technique close to the vest until you've perfected it, or patented or copyrighted it. Sometimes that innovation will bear your name.

It is said that Eddie Van Halen (yes, I am a huge EVH fan) used to turn his back to the audience during solos so his innovative two-handed tapping technique couldn't copied. Eventually he showed his stuff and the result has been a generation of guitar players who've done amazing things. My point is that when you make your ideas available to others, you haven't lost anything. Instead, you've made a contribution and have solidified your legacy.

Teachers and Their Impact

Teachers have made a huge impact on me. I've mentioned Jo Shapiro, M.D., whom I still call on for advice. My senior partner, Bjorn Bie, M.D., has great insights into medicine and life in general, and has been a mentor. But there are three teachers whose influence has been especially profound. Here are "the big three" in chronological order.

Mrs. Rose Lester was my sixth-grade teacher. She taught us to be proud of our differences, to embrace them, and foster them.

Remember your elementary school days. Wasn't it important to be cool? Was it cool to be smart? I was a fat, brainy, geeky kid, barely athletic, with thick glasses. I had acne and had to shave before the other kids did. I played violin and upright bass. Not too many kids back then wanted to be like Beethoven or Bach. (I kept my guitar playing under wraps.) I felt like an outsider. I was teased and bullied. (Bullying didn't get the attention in the '70s that it does today.) My father taught me not to back down, so I could defend myself pretty well. But you know what? I would have traded every single A to, just once, not be the last person picked for a team. Mrs. Lester taught me not be embarrassed about being smart.

She saw something good in all of us. She protected and encouraged the impoverished girl who wore the same clothes to school every day and made it clear we had no right to tease her. She helped the class clown/bully realize he had qualities worth fostering. From her I learned the concept of defining and celebrating my own successes.

Mrs. Rose Lester seemed religious and sometimes quoted from the *Bible*. To the young girl she said, "Remember what Jesus said when he was on the cross, 'Forgive them Father, for they know not what they do.'" She wanted that girl to remember that phrase any time she was bullied, and be better than her bullies.

Mrs. Lester had some great expressions. When we acted immature, she'd say, "You'll have a lot more responsibility and you won't find this stuff funny when you start smelling yourself." The phrase "when you start smelling yourself" referred to hitting puberty when your cute prepubescent aroma turned into hair-curling adolescent sweat.

Mrs. Lester was also my first African-American (or African-Canadian) teacher. Our school was in a white, blue-collar neighborhood. At International Day when we celebrated our heritage, we learned that 49% of the class had Irish heritage, 49% Italian, and 2% Polish/German/Lithuanian. All were white. Mrs. Lester was, I think, married to a white man, which raised eyebrows in the '70s. It must have taken guts to teach in that setting, yet she was undaunted. She believed in celebrating uniqueness, in overcoming prejudice, in showing us that we were all special.

She introduced us to the idea of multiculturalism, a new part of the school curriculum. She opened our eyes and minds to understanding others' strengths regardless of race, religion, or gender. I thank you, Mrs. Lester, wherever you are, for showing me it's all right to be unique, to not be ashamed or embarrassed to stand out or question the status quo. You taught us to stand up to prejudice, and you were ahead of the curve in teaching us to not tolerate bullying. I knew, even in sixth grade, that Mrs. Lester was a woman of great fortitude who believed in herself. Her role went beyond sixth-grade teacher. She was a teacher of life.

My high-school math teacher at Malden Catholic, Brother Fred Eid, had a huge influence on me. He was also my homeroom teacher for a year, my junior varsity soccer coach, the math team advisor, and my freshman algebra teacher and senior calculus BC teacher. He loved math and had a passion for teaching.

He had the same passion for school events, especially soccer: the game itself, and teaching it. He was passionate about math meets, where teams of "mathletes" from various schools competed. We loved discussing math theories, equations, algorithms, formulas, and problem-solving strategies. In one meet I got a perfect score—all questions correct, 18 points. He was so proud.

Brother Eid also taught me that sometimes the student becomes the teacher. One day in homeroom the four or five students running for homeroom representatives gave speeches as to why they should be elected. An Asian student spoke. Then another student made his case and said something like, "And anyway, you don't want some ch*nk to represent our homeroom."

> *Sometimes the student becomes the teacher.*

I remember the shock on Brother Eid's face. He talked about the inappropriateness of that remark. What impressed me was later that day, he called me into his office and asked, "What did you think about what happened today in homeroom?" I told him I was shocked. He said when it happened he was at a loss about what to do. In that moment, he and I were colleagues. He asked me to discuss with the other students the inappropriateness of that behavior.

Brother Eid eventually left the Xaverian Brothers and recently passed away from a brain tumor. I thank him for teaching me to be passionate, for showing me that teachers can learn from their students, and that we can learn together. I learned teacher and student have an important bond and create an effective team that, based on mutual respect, can accomplish great things.

Dr. William Silen, Johnson and Johnson Professor of Surgery (Emeritus), Harvard Medical School, profoundly influenced me.

He was the Chief of Surgery at Beth Israel Hospital in Boston when I was an intern.

When I matched for residency at the Massachusetts Eye and Ear Infirmary/Harvard Medical School Otolaryngology program, I had to do a year-long surgical internship (general surgery) first. Staff at the academic office at Mass. Eye and Ear explained my program options and I asked their advice. They said that Dr. Joseph Nadol, the Chief of Otolaryngology at Mass. Eye and Ear (an outstanding teacher and mentor and who taught me otologic/ear surgery in residency) had done his internship at Beth Israel, so I said, "Sign me up."

Students at Boston University said, "You're doing your internship at Beth Israel? Good luck. Dr. Silen makes you round at 3:30 a.m. You'll be on call every other night. He hates all people going into ENT. He's impossible to please." And so on.

But I've never been afraid of hard work or a challenge. I was ready to work my butt off, and often worked with Dr. Silen. Was he tough? Yes! Was he demanding? Yes! And was he amazing and awesome? Yes! Dr. Silen cared about his patients.

We had to call Dr. Silen every night at 8 p.m. and discuss each patient's condition and our plans for the overnight treatment. At 5 a.m. we met with him. If there were a lot of patients, we had to get up around 3:30 a.m. to pre-round on all of them. We checked how they were feeling, their vital signs, their medication lists to see what medications were ordered (or stopped), and how much pain medication they'd gotten and when. We checked how their incision looked or their belly felt, and how their intravenous sites looked in case there was inflammation that might cause a fever. We paid attention to every detail.

Dr. Silen's surgery was meticulous and virtually bloodless. He paid attention to every preoperative, intraoperative, and postoperative detail to make the surgery thoughtful and efficient, ensuring the best possible care.

Dr. Silen was a great teacher. I learned that attention to detail improved patient care and saved time chasing down details on rounds. He taught the importance of punctuality in medicine and in life, and the value of our patients' time and our colleagues' time. He was never late for a clinic or meeting, and expected the same of us.

If he was tough on us, it was because he was tough on himself. He wanted each of us as interns, residents, and staff physicians to hold ourselves to the highest standards. He was never complacent about his knowledge or abilities. He had a dry sense of humor, called radiologists "coupon clippers" and endocrinologists "endocriminologists." When I did something he didn't like, he'd say "You'll do great at the Eye and Ear—you're operating like a real nose picker."

He taught us that we needed excellent visualization (exposure) when operating, that we shouldn't stick our fingers blindly into an anatomic area when operating, because our fingers don't have eyes. If we got into complications because we stuck our fingers into a blood vessel or a visceral structure without adequate exposure, he'd bend his index finger toward us, move it side to side, and ask, "Did you use the finger with the eye?"

He taught that everything we do to or for patients has consequences. We need to analyze and evaluate, and be accountable. If we order tests, we act on them and follow up on the results. If we order treatments or medications, then order other ones to counteract consequences of the first, we reevaluate why we did the first treatment or gave the initial medications.

I faced Dr. Silen's wrath a few times. One day we were to meet at 5 a.m. on Feldberg 7, a floor at Beth Israel, for morning rounds. We did "gravity rounds," that is, we started at the highest floor then worked down. I'd called him the night before as usual. After that phone call, the patient on Feldberg 7 had been moved to another floor because of bed space issues. I didn't want to call Dr. Silen late at night for something not related to patient care, so I figured we'd meet on Feldberg 7. But at 5 a.m., Dr. Silen wasn't there. At 5:10, still no Dr. Silen. At 5:25 a.m., no Dr. Silen. We were getting worried. At 5:30, Dr. Silen entered the nurses' station, and we were relieved. Then, as they say, he laid into me.

Remember the attention to detail I mentioned above? When Dr. Silen got to the hospital he apparently checked the patient's location and at 5 a.m. sharp, went to the new floor, expecting us to be there. We weren't, and he was mad. He said we'd lost half an hour of teaching. He called me and what I'd done "stupid" a thousand times that morning. In surgical residency we were expected to do our best and be on our toes. I wasn't upset with Dr. Silen, but with myself.

Another time I met with Dr. Silen for rounds. We had to report to the Breast Clinic about a half hour after rounds, so got breakfast in the cafeteria. Then I decided I needed a shower. I strolled into the Breast Clinic about 10 minutes late. (In medical school, residents ran a lot of clinics at the city hospital. The residents were often late. I'd come to think that was the norm.) Dr. Silen was unhappy. I'd kept a patient waiting for 10 minutes and delayed the rest of the schedule. The lesson: being late disrespected other people's time.

One day Dr. Silen said, "Step into my orifice and pull up a loose stool." He was pleased with my progress and said I must study a lot (I did; still do). He asked point blank whether I read in the bathroom, sitting on the toilet. I admitted it. He said, "You're going to get Silen's Syndrome." I looked at him. What had I missed? Was this in the book he'd edited, Cope's Early Diagnosis of the Acute Abdomen (Oxford University Press, latest revision 2005)? Then he smiled and said, "You know, Silen's syndrome. Nearsightedness and hemorrhoids." Then he showed me a letter he'd written to Dr. Nadol, Chief of Otolaryngology at Mass. Eye and Ear, praising my work at Beth Israel. The letter concluded, "We tried to convince Arthur that he had too much on the ball to be an otolaryngologist ..." I'm surprised he didn't say "nose picker," and that he didn't call me "Ahtha." He never let me live down my Boston accent.

What a great guy Dr. Silen is. He didn't have to write to Dr. Nadol, but he did it anyway. He said I "read avidly" and that I was "truly an exceptional and real doctor." He put the patient first, hence his tough demands and high standards. When I watched him sit with patients, examine them, speak with them, operate on them, and care for them and their families, I felt an overwhelming atmosphere of compassion. This carried over into his love for teaching, for making his students better doctors.

Dr. Silen taught me to set high standards, that it's okay to demand a lot from others when you're demanding of yourself. Never be complacent. Strive to do better, to improve, so you can help others. You're always a student. Even as chief of surgery, you can always learn more. Respect the time of others—be punctual. And most important: however demanding you are, always be compassionate. I can't thank Dr. Silen enough for his influence on my career and on my life.

I've had many other great teachers in all aspects of my life. I have such gratitude for their passion and their generosity. My cousin Andrea teaches elementary school and is working on a Masters in Education. Her students love her. She devotes countless hours to making each school year special for her students. With her advanced degrees, she'll be able to offer even more to her students and her community. I admire her energy and her dedication.

> *We never know when the simplest act of teaching may blossom into a huge opportunity for one of our students.*

Teachers give in the same way doctors take care of patients. Think about an elementary school teacher with a class of 25. She cares for and teaches each child for six hours a day as if the child were her own. Most teachers I know stay after school and come in before school to give kids extra help. Teachers volunteer generously, running activities after school and on weekends. This dedication is what makes teaching so valuable. It recognizes that our students are our future.

Unfortunately, teachers' salaries don't come close to their value to society. But as I've said, there are more important rewards than financial ones. We never know when the simplest act of teaching may blossom into a huge opportunity for one of our students.

Role Models and Responsibilities

Wikipedia defines role model as a "person who serves as an example, whose behavior is emulated by others."

Do you think you're a role model? Have you set a goal to be one, or are you one by chance? The reality is, we may be role models and not know it. Kids usually view their parents as role models.

Unfortunately, not all parents are positive ones. Maybe they abuse their spouses or children, or engage in dangerous or self-destructive behavior. Many had parents who did the same to them. One expert estimates that 40% of sexual abusers were sexually abused as children (Vanderbilt, 1992), and children of alcoholics are four times more likely than others to develop alcoholism (some genetic factors may be at play). The point is, children emulate our behaviors, good and bad.

As a kid I often heard, "Actions speak louder than words." When I did something my parents did that wasn't good for me, I'd say, "Well, you do it." Take smoking. Some of my aunts and uncles smoked heavily, and some have died from complications from smoking. So when I said, "Smoking must be okay. You do it," they retorted, "Do as I say, not as I do."

We are role models, whether we want to be or not. We may want people to emulate some of what we do. The problem is, we don't have control over what others do. If we're in the public eye—not just celebrities, but politicians, physicians, teachers, lawyers, police officers, firefighters, and so on—people will, in one way or another, see us as role models. So we need to be aware of our strengths and weaknesses and be open about them with our would-be protégés.

Our culture has double standards for role models. Highly visible people are often held to higher standards. Say the store manager of a flower shop in town is arrested for driving under the influence of alcohol (DUI)—no accident, and no one was injured. This appears in the police log in the town paper, and you probably won't see it. But if the town mayor does the same thing, you might see it on the front page. When a U.S. Senator does it, it makes the national news. If our activities appear negative, we'll need to be ready to answer questions.

Even criminals can be role models. Look at Oliver Stone's Natural Born Killers (1994) with Woody Harrelson and Juliette Lewis. The media glorifies a serial-killer couple.

How Do We Choose?

Over the years I've learned many techniques from other surgeons, but that doesn't mean every one is good for my practice. I have to be selective, filter what's relevant—what works, and what doesn't. I've worked with surgeons and said, "That was a great way to remove that tumor. I'm going to remember that." But I'm not going to emulate their poor bedside manner.

My role models include people who continually seek to improve what they do. We can all be perpetual students. We're never too old to learn, never too far along in our careers to learn new skills. I've had patients in their 70s and 80s who were taking courses at local universities. I heard a news story about a woman who started guitar lessons at age 60. It was her lifelong dream.

I was intrigued by an article by the skilled and renowned surgeon, Atul Gawande, M.D., in The New Yorker (October 3, 2011) titled "Personal Best." Dr. Gawande notes that in his eight years as a surgeon, he continued to get better and better results, with his complication rate falling below the national average. Then his level of improvement began to plateau. So he engaged a coach, a senior surgeon who could observe his procedures and make suggestions. This was his opportunity learn more and improve, to the benefit of his patients.

Doctors and nurses are required to continue their education to maintain their licenses. Lifelong learning can involve any topic or skill—speaking to others who share your interests, or going to a local community college or a seminar at a church or library.

We can learn from experts who are older and have more experience, but in medicine, those younger than we are may have a greater knowledge of a new technique. By the time I was a chief resident, I'd done more endoscopic sinus surgery procedures (a new technique at the time) than many attendings. So when we residents scrubbed on a sinus case with such an attending, we demonstrated newer techniques. I've learned new guitar techniques from younger players and martial arts techniques from people half my age. The human mind needs stimulation, and it benefits from new challenges and the continued quest for knowledge. Learn something new!

Your Legacy

In summary: Each generation benefits from the lessons of previous generations. History has much to teach us. We have an obligation to pass on wisdom to the next generation. Students who improve on their teachers reward them and affirm their ability to educate and motivate. When we're always learning, the possibilities of what we can do become infinite. By continuing to grow in knowledge, we can continue to make the world a better place. When we pass on this knowledge, we leave a legacy that helps the next generation make society better. When we give future generations the building blocks to create new opportunities, they see that opportunities to teach and learn are opportunities to do the right thing.

> *When we're always learning, the possibilities of what we can do become infinite.*

Chapter Thirteen:
PUTTING IT ALL TOGETHER

How do we put this all together? *What does it mean to do the right thing?* My ideas are based on the premise that there is a "right thing" and that we are capable of doing it. I believe, and I hope I've convinced you, that *we are able* to help others, make a positive impact on society, and avoid prejudice, and instead, celebrate our differences and uniqueness. We are able to make good first impressions and recognize the talents we all possess. I believe we have an innate desire to make this world a better place, and pass on our legacy through the gift of teaching.

For me, one word is of paramount importance when we discuss the idea of doing the right thing. I've deliberately not used this word (except once in the dedication), so I present it now—the ace up my sleeve.

The word is *integrity.* Consider these definitions:

• Dictionary.com: "adherence to moral and ethical principles; soundness of moral character; honesty."

• Wikipedia: "a concept of consistency of actions, values, methods, measures, principles, expectations, and outcomes …"

• *Encarta World English Dictionary* (2009, Microsoft): the "possession of firm principles; the quality of possessing and steadfastly adhering to *high* moral principles or professional standards." (Italics mine.)

Having integrity means adhering to a set of moral and ethical principles that benefit those around us, and contribute to society.

I've emphasized being your own person and defining success in your own terms. The fact is, though, others judge whether we're persons of integrity. I can tell you until I'm blue in the face that I'm a person of integrity. But I don't get to decide that. What matters is how others judge my words, actions, and character. I do believe we can define what it means to be a person of integrity.

An intrinsic part of integrity is honesty—with others and ourselves. Even when no one witnesses our actions, we stick to our moral code, our principles, and do the right thing. This value system runs counter to the saying, "It's only illegal if you get caught." When we do the right thing for its own sake, we feel a sense of accomplishment.

A poem I recommend gets to the heart of being a person of integrity. Mother Teresa's 'The Final Analysis" is based on the poem "Anyway," posted on the wall of her Children's Home in Calcutta. According to Wowzone.com, it contained eight of Kent M. Keith's 10 "Paradoxical Commandments" from his 1968 booklet for student leaders titled *The Silent Revolution: Dynamic Leadership in the Student Council.* It concludes "... in the final analysis, it is between you and God." In this last stanza, we can replace "it is between you and God" with "it is between you and the greater good, " or "it is between you and your conscience." The point is, this can apply to all of us, whether or whomever we worship.

Recall in the chapter on teaching I mentioned that our parents say, "Be a leader, not a follower," then turn around and ask, "Why can't you be like the other kids?" These seemingly opposing statements make sense in context. They both model integrity. We follow the crowd when the crowd is, say, working with Habitat for Humanity to build a new home for an underprivileged family, and we also stand up against the crowd when we help someone who's being bullied.

Conscience

We can view conscience as the ethical barometer or moral guide that resides somewhere in the recesses of our brains, hearts, and souls. It is intangible, yet present. It's the voice in our heads that we talk to or debate when we're assessing whether something is right or wrong, and whether we should act based on what we believe is right or wrong.

We may ascribe aspects of our conscience to our religious beliefs and teachings, or to the societal norms of right and wrong. We learn these norms as children, then through our culture, education, experience, and so on. Conscience can develop in spite of these norms. Maybe we grew up in a culture of prejudice, then over time our conscience, or innate sense of right and wrong, led us to reverse our views. We may learn a lot from our environment, but I believe understanding right and wrong is to some degree innate.

When my daughter was around two, she was obsessed with the Disney video *Pinocchio* and the characters of The Blue Fairy and Jiminy Cricket. She called it "NO-key-no," and would have watched it three or four times a day. As Pinocchio's surrogate conscience, Jiminy Cricket describes conscience as "that still, small voice that people won't listen to. That's just the trouble with the world today."

Given my choices of quotations (Dr. Seuss and now a Disney character), you may be questioning my sanity, but Jiminy Cricket is right about conscience and right to say we don't always listen. Sometimes we see right and wrong in narrow terms. Think of typical teenage questions: "Should I smoke? Should I try drugs?" We've heard about the immoral and unethical behavior of people who are tempted by the terms of wills or inheritances or the allure of "victimless" white-collar crimes. Sometimes choosing right over wrong can be difficult.

We can view conscience as the ethical barometer or moral guide that resides somewhere in the recesses of our brains, hearts, and souls.

We may not get immediate gratification when we do the right thing. I love the immediate gratification of being a surgeon, of removing a tumor. But sometimes surgery is not the answer, and chemotherapy and radiation are the better treatments. I need to wait and see whether the cancer begins to shrink. In the same way, when we help others, the effort will eventually pay off.

A Social Impulse

The desire to help others, to do unto others, is a major driver in the progression of society and is, to some degree, innate and satisfying because we've learned that working together, supporting each other, and having a positive impact ensure the survival of a civilized society. The "do unto others" philosophy may be a survival instinct. Perhaps this is why helping someone *feels so good!*

Is our desire to do good innate? That question has been subject to debate for centuries. The English philosophers and social contract theorists John Locke and Thomas Hobbes held opposing views. Hobbes (1588—1679) wrote *Leviathan*, in which he described man's life as "solitary, poor, nasty, brutish, and short." We are incapable of knowing good and evil, and without the oversight of a sovereign power, will fall into chaos. We see this in William Golding's Lord of the Flies (1954), where a group of British boys stranded on an island try to govern themselves and sink into savagery.

In contrast is John Locke (1632—1704), who believed that the state of nature was not a state of war but a state of peace. He believed humans understood right and wrong, and would cooperate with each other because they saw themselves as equal—the reciprocity we speak of in the philosophy "do unto others."

Call me an optimist, but with Locke, I believe we do understand right and wrong and we are driven to do good things and help others, because that's how we want to be treated. We find it truly gratifying. Perhaps I'm a sentimental optimist, even an idealist, but my hope is that such good exists. It's largely this hope that is behind the ideas in this book.

I've talked a lot about my medical career and ideas from it we can apply to situations in our lives. The surgeon's life involves integrity, honesty, transparency, and commitment to helping others. We must do the right thing even when it's difficult or may not be acknowledged, or when the only gain is the satisfaction of helping others. Doing no harm, avoiding prejudice, making a good first impression, contributing to society, and having a positive impact are all part of the surgeon's role, along with the responsibility to teach and pass on our legacy. These principles apply to all of us, no matter what we do. Society blossoms and flourishes when we work together to make life better for everyone.

For me, being a good person means that, in most cases, I have to stay within the lines of the "coloring book of life," the rules and norms to which I adhere. I do many surgical cases in a standard fashion because that's the standard of care. The same is true for much of life. But sometimes we have to veer outside the lines. Sometimes I have applied a well-known, time-tested surgical procedure to a case or situation that does not usually call for that procedure. It's a bit scary at first, but the results have usually been gratifying. We make progress when we think outside the box and move outside the lines, perhaps questioning an institution, not to disband it or topple it over, but to question the *status quo*.

Unions are an example. Unions formed not because people didn't want to work—they didn't want to work in terrible conditions. Child labor laws disrupted an unthinkable status quo—children were being exploited. Sometimes integrity drives us way outside the lines. We have to tear out a page or start drawing an entirely different picture. Think about the abolition of slavery and equal rights for women. Sometimes we have to start with a blank canvas to effect positive change and do the right thing.

At the end of Steven Spielberg's *Saving Private Ryan*, I cried like a baby. On the bridge at Ramelle, Captain John H. Miller (Tom Hanks), as he is dying, tells Private First Class James Francis Ryan (Matt Damon), "James... earn this. Earn it." The scene changes to the present day, when a now much-older James Francis Ryan is in front of Captain Miller's grave. Ryan says to the gravestone, "Every day I think about what you said to me that day on the bridge. And I've tried to live my life the best I could. I hope that was enough. I hope that at least in your eyes, I've earned what all of you have done for me." His wife reads the gravestone. Then Ryan says to his wife, "Tell me I've led a good life. Tell me I'm a good man." Imagine being in Ryan's shoes. Imagine that others have given their lives so you can live yours.

At that point in the movie I wondered, Have I been the best person I could be? Have I tried to make a difference for others, to have a positive impact on those around me and perhaps others far beyond my immediate community? I wondered how often I'd asked myself, Have I led a good life? Am I a good man, a good person, a person of integrity? This is powerful stuff. After that movie, I began periodically reflecting on the things I've done. Have I been someone others would see as a person of integrity?

> *Sometimes integrity drives us way outside the lines. We have to tear out a page or start drawing an entirely different picture.*

As we go through life we weave what I think of as a moral fabric. This is the value system we create and adhere to, the rules we follow that we believe will benefit others, the positive impact we make, our contributions, and our legacy.

If you were to display your moral fabric, the cloth you've woven, what would it be? Would it be a rich, thick tapestry, the tapestry of a person of integrity? Would it be a strong cloth, but one with some areas of wear or some holes, where at times you didn't have a positive impact? Or would it be a wispy, gossamer veil, easily shredded and torn?

Call me the optimist, but I think most of us weave a richer tapestry than we give ourselves credit for. If our moral fabric is strong but has holes, we can repair those holes and still end up with the moral fabric of those who do the right thing.

I close this book with my original statement. People have often asked me, "What makes surgeons do the things they do? What makes us do the right thing in a given situation?" The gratification I get from helping others is what drives me as a surgeon, and I believe it drives all of us because we're inherently good and we care about others. We have the capacity to do good things, great things, the right things. We need to believe in this capacity, and exercise it often.

I've shared my perspectives and the lessons I've learned with the hope that they'll be helpful to you. Like everyone else, I'm still striving—and at times struggling—to do the right thing.

I strive to be seen as a person of integrity. When I look at my moral and ethical tapestry, I'm honest enough to see the holes. I'd like to think they were made a long time ago, and that life has taught me how to repair them and prevent new ones. But I still have a long way to go in my quest to do the right thing.

Life is a journey and the destination is not always clear. When we reach one destination, we usually look at the horizon and seek a new one. So it is with our quest to do the right thing. This quest is a work in progress, but our successes will far outweigh the failures.

And what's important about our failures is how we respond to them, how we turn them into successes. This is what makes the journey so exciting and gratifying. The realization that we are doing the right thing makes the journey of life a wonderful adventure.

I offer these final words of encouragement in your journey to do the right thing. Dr. Seuss ended his book *Oh, the Places You'll Go!* with the words, "Today is your day! Your mountain is waiting. So... *get on your way!*" I encourage you to recognize you've already done much good. Take pride in that. And know you will have more opportunities to help others, contribute to society, make the world a better place, and pass on your legacy.

I hope you have found some of my insights helpful, and I thank you for giving them consideration. I'm positive you have what it takes to be a person of integrity. Now, go out there and *do the right thing!*

ARTHUR LAURETANO

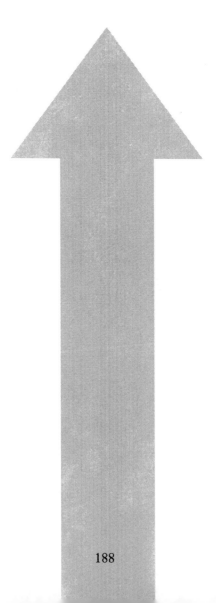

Chapter Fourteen:
AFTERTHOUGHTS

In some respects, this book is for people who feel they help others or "do the right thing," but often stop to wonder why. Perhaps they don't feel their efforts are appreciated or respected, or perhaps they feel their efforts mean little or have little effect. This book says, "You are making a difference. Your efforts are worthwhile. Keep up the good work." I've had these same concerns.

Writing this book has been incredibly enlightening for me—even cathartic. I've subscribed to the ideas in this book for a long time, many for my entire life. Sometimes I've felt that others were getting ahead in life and seemed to have it easier. Such thinking caused me to ask, "Why? Why am I a physician? Why do I make the extra effort? Why do others seem to get farther ahead when I'm working just as hard?" I've looked at people I've treated or who've suffered great hardships and asked the old question, "Why do bad things happen to good people?" Such concerns led me to see a therapist, Joe Erickson.

> *I've looked at people I've treated or who've suffered great hardships and asked the old question, "Why do bad things happen to good people?"*

I'd already started to think about and write down a lot of the thoughts in this book. Once I began to discuss these issues with my therapist, I felt a great sense of relief and confidence in my beliefs and convictions. That inspired me to put these thoughts into this book. Writing it was enlightening, because I could go back and read my ideas and principles. Sometimes reading the ideas gave me insight. At other times, my own errors were glaringly obvious. And sometimes I felt that passing my ideas on was in keeping with my desire to help others and to teach.

Sometimes I thought, "Wow, some people are going to think I'm a real wimp or don't have that tough persona attributed to surgeons." But I stuck to my belief in the premises in "The Final Analysis" and wrote it anyway.

Maybe you disagree with me. But if I made you think, or sparked some interest in these subjects, even if you reached different conclusions, I feel I've accomplished something. I've made sure I've been true to my principles and reaffirmed my belief in them. I believe in practicing what I preach. And in so doing, I believe I'm doing the right thing.

THANK YOU FOR READING MY BOOK!

Visit me at www.drarthurlauretano.com and follow me on Twitter: @drlauretano. Let me know your stories and comments.

More ways to help:

- Please consider writing a review and posting it at your point of purchase. As an author, I rely on you, my readers, to help me get the word out. You'll help me out in a big way if you take a few minutes to write a review.

- By telling others how you benefited from *Do the Right Thing*, you'll be helping them redefine their priorities and focus on doing the right thing. You'll have my eternal gratitude.

For updates, advance notice about future promotions, giveaways and other benefits, visit www.drarthurlauretano.com and join the *Do the Right Thing* mailing list!

ABOUT THE AUTHOR

Arthur M. Lauretano, M.D., M.S., F.A.C.S., an otolaryngologist-head and neck surgeon, is currently the Medical Director of the Multidisciplinary Head and Neck Cancer Center and the Medical Director of Inpatient Specialty Services at Lowell General Hospital. He has been a clinical instructor at Harvard Medical School and teaches Boston University otolaryngology residents at the Lahey Clinic.

The only child of a carpenter and a homemaker, he grew up in Medford, Massachusetts. He was valedictorian of Malden Catholic High School, graduated from the Boston University Six-Year Medical Program, and completed his otolaryngology residency at Harvard Medical School. Arthur also has a Master's degree in Healthcare Administration and Clinical Informatics from the University of Massachusetts Lowell. A proud computer and math geek, he lives in a suburb of Boston with his wife Adrienne, his daughter Danielle the animator, and his son Arthur the aspiring artist. Arthur is also a professional guitarist, a second degree black belt in Kyusho-Kempo karate, and is passionate about soccer.